A *Woman's* MENTAL OBSESSION

A *Woman's* MENTAL OBSESSION

ZANETA CANNON ROBINSON

Z.Z. THAT AUTHOR

Ordering Information:

For orders and inquiries, please contact:
1-888-404-1388
www.goldtouchpress.com
book.orders@goldtouchpress.com

Printed in the United States of America

DEDICATION

"LONG LIVE BEAN CANNON-MANSELL"

MY BOOK IS DEDICATED to my mother Vernetta "Bean" Cannon-Mansell. My world got flipped upside down January 8th, 2021. My mother died; she had been suffering from COPD since 2012. Her condition had deteriorated over the years. She pushed an oxygen tank around and dispensed several medications throughout the years to help pro-long her life. She gave this disease the fight of her life. She did not give up she gave out. The struggle became too much to handle, and God seen fit to call her home. My brother, son and I were deeply devastated by her passing. The doctors had been trying to prepare us for that day for years, but you can never be ready. There is no preparation for the death of your mother. Making funeral arrangements and having to bury your mother is not for the weak. Losing my mother has opened a new window on life for me. Live, laugh, love is the best I can describe it, life is too short to be on some negativity and not try to be productive. My mom always taught my brother and I to aim for success, the sky is the limit and there is always room for improvement. She always told me to hold my head up high after making a mistake, learn from it and keep it pushing. Life is so joyous and a blessing to be amongst the ones you love. Watching my mother slip away from me was the hardest thing I ever had to face.

I was raised by the best and was taught things that will always be instilled in my head. My mom gave me so much knowledge on the fakeness and unloyalty of people, and that lesson came to light when she took sick. Her own family vanished away like a thief in the night during her time of need. It made me sick to my stomach knowing all my mom had done for people and she was getting treated like an outcast. My brother, son and I along with her special group of friends made sure she had the best of everything and gave her exactly what she wanted during her last days of living. There has not ever been a time to where I did not have my mom. From my childhood to my teen life, and my adult life my mom has been right by my side rocking and rolling. She was the frick to my frack and the ying to my yang. I miss my mom so much and I still cry to this day, the pain is real, and it runs deep through my soul. My world is lonely without her, she will always live on in my heart and I will never let her memory or legacy die. My mom was an icon to people, she touched so many lives with her tell it like it is ways she never sugar coated anything. The best cook, the best dressed, and the most beautiful lady that you could have ever met. It was a complete honor to have been raised by such a phenomenal woman. It's natural for every human being to love their mom, but the way my loves run for my mom is never ending, it is so indescribable. I love hard just like the pain is hard to bear without her. I will hold on to our memories and dance to your favorite song "BEFORE I LET GO" every time I hear it. REST EASY MOMMY, MY QUEEN BEAN. I love you for ETERNITY...........

Mrs. Vernetta Cannon-Mansell
2/9/1956 - 1/8/2021

Happy
Mother's
Day!
VERNETTA CANNON-MANSELL
FEB. 9
1956
JAN. 8
2021

x

DISCLAIMER

This story is not about any induvial at hand. This is a fiction story. The characters and chapters of this story were made up by the author. This story is not targeted towards any individual with a mental illness. The author is not downplaying the seriousness of mental illness in no way. She and all her camp understand the severity of mental illness and its effects on the men, women, and children of the world. This manuscript is not meant to make fun of or pick at anyone suffering from mental issues. The author would like to encourage all her readers to use all local resources to maintain mental stability. Mental health issues are on the rise, especially during the current state of the world, check on your friends and family to make sure they are ok and well. If you know someone suffering from an unstable mental issue, seek them some help, you could very well save a life by doing so. Be blessed and thank you for reading.

SINCERELY, Z.Z. THAT AUTHOR
SAMHSA'S NATIONAL HELPLINE
1-800-662-HELP (4357)
FREE & CONFIDENTIAL 24/7 365 DAYS-A-YEAR
ENGLISH & SPANISH

CONTENTS

Chapter 1

THE START UP

DONALD MURPHY IS A college freshman at Upstate University, in Anderson SC. Donald never knew he could make it to college. The neighborhood he grew up in rarely had success stories. Donald always had potential and was extremely smart, his grades were awesome, and he stayed on the Dean's list.

Donald had several different talents, and he managed success with them all. Donald was not perfect and at times fell short. These times in his life he was following behind his older brother Alvin. An earthly giant standing an even 7 feet, Alvin once had a love for the game of basketball but like a lot of young boys in their community he was turned out by the streets. Some of the street boys in the neighborhood convinced him to start hustling and he took to it like a duck takes to water. Alvin quickly became King of the streets and openly enjoyed all that came with the title he had been given. Especially the night life. The street life was not for Donald and everyone knew that, however Donald felt the need to be around his brother no matter the cost. Even with the years between them, their bond was like that of twins, undeniable, unbreakable. Vernetta, their mom, always blamed Alvin whenever Donald got in trouble. "You are your brother's keeper and right now you are keeping him in trouble!", she would scream whenever the news of Donald being wild and crazy came home. Their mom pushed Donald everyday to be great and do the right thing. For the longest she did not think she was getting through to him. Unbeknownst to her Alvin was also pushing his brother to do and be the best things possible in life.

She finally began to see results of all her encouragement when Donald was awarded a full scholarship in art.

He was an amazingly talented artist. Donald had been drawing since kindergarten and by the time he got to grade school he was damn near a Picasso. With his brother's help, Donald was able to make a lucrative business drawing tattoos and painting portraits. He later taught himself to use the actual tattoo gun. He had to make money some kind of way, Alvin refused to let him sale drugs. "Hell, nah lil nigga! Mamma aint finna kill me. Besides you better than thi shit. Hustle your talents D. Let me be the bad guy", Alvin would say. So, Donald made a name for himself throughout high school and by the time he made it to college he was the go-to man for tattoos. His mom would curse and threaten him about all this extra money, accusing Alvin of having her baby caught up in the streets. She did not believe that is how he got all his money until she saw first had how good he was and how much clientele he had. Spring Break of his junior year in high school Donald wanted to go with his friends to Panama City but his mom did not have the money. Alvin and Donald hosted a tattoo party at the house and Donald walked away with five thousand dollars. Before he left for his trip Ms. Vernetta took him downtown to fill out all the paperwork to make him a legit business owner. She knew he was special and wanted him to be the only person to capitalize off his efforts and talents. Donald was always busy, but he started finding time to entertain a young lady, Courtney Mimms.

The two had been classmates most of their school career but once in high school they ended up in the majority of their classes together. They always ended up being partners for projects and labs. School partners led to lunch partners and friends. This friendship quickly grew into a young romance, and soon the two were inseparable. By the time graduation came around the two were in love and planning a life together. Courtney waws just as smart and talented as Donald so the two were considered "Couple Goals" for their peers. In the Senior yearbook for superlatives the two were voted "Jay-Z and Beyonce" of the school, along with most Popular, most likely to succeed, and they even were crowned prom king and queen for their class. They always motivated and supported one another, not just when it came to themselves as a couple but in life and anything they decided to do. College was no different, Courtney was in Greenville, SC while Donald stayed in Anderson, SC. Although 45 minutes apart the two remained solid and in love. They pushed each other and they graduated early, choosing to work in their perspective fields of choice. Donald expanded his tattoo business with the help of Courtney, having two shops, one in Greenville and the original location in Anderson. He also opened an upscale art gallery. Courtney became a social worker for Greenville County DSS.

It was a childhood dream of hers. Her passion stemmed from her childhood and the situation she and her siblings were placed in. The woman that she called mom was really her birth mother's best friend. For reasons unknown to Courtney or her sisters, their mom left them one day and never returned. She counted herself lucky to have the family and people in her life that loved her enough to make sure she did not go without. However, she knew that most kids do not get a fairytale ending and need someone to advocate for them. She was determined to be that advocate.

Shondrella Hicks, a beautiful young lady with curves that would stop traffic and turn all heads, male and female, was working at Ralph Hicks and Associates Law firm. Shondrella was unstable as they came but her mother and family tried to keep her sane with medication and a normal schedule. Ralph being her uncle decided to help by giving her a job. She was tasked with decorating one of the conference rooms and decided she needed artwork for the walls. Trusting her, Ralph gave Shondrella a company card and told her to go get what she needed. Donald's art gallery was almost directly across the street so Shondrella sashayed on over to see what she could find. Upon entry the door chimed, and she was greeted with the most beautiful smile she had ever seen.

"Good afternoon ma'am.", extending his hand for a shake, "I am Donald Murphy, and I will be happy to help you". She shook his hand and immediately began flirting asking unnecessary questions about the artwork. Shondrella made sure to let him know what she was looking for, in a man and in the artwork as well. Being the professional that he was, Donald kept it polite and strictly business. While ignoring her obvious advances, Donald was explaining which pieces he felt would best fit the office she was decorating. He noticed drool seeping from the corner of her mouth and knew that something was off about her, so he ended the conversation by excusing himself. "Ms. Hicks if would please excuse me I have to get going, but my staff can further assist you with anything here." Before he could finish, he noticed that Shondrella had started to zone out and her tongue was slightly hanging from her mouth. Not wanting to be rude or make this anymore awkward he left. "If you desire a custom piece, please fill out the paperwork and it will be delivered for you", he walked away. Shondrella nodded her head in acknowledgement but her eyes were full of lust. He was her man, and they were in love. That was all there was to it.

To the any passerby Shondrella appeared totally normal. She had several issues, but they were not visible until she had an episode. Her biggest issue was delusions, but she was clinically diagnosed with Bipolar Schizophrenia Disorder, and dissociative identity disorder. She would get fixated on a person or a thing and her mind would take it from there. Shondrella's weakness was men. She never had her father or the affection of a father figure, so she constantly sought out the attention and love from one. She planned a fairytale in her head and was simply looking for prince charming to play his role. The last guy, Emory, barley got away from her. Emory reached out to the local authorities, but after no luck with the restraining orders, and no trespassing orders, he was fed up with her bullshit.

Shondrella caused so much damage and heartache in his life, he refused to continue to live his life this way. Out of desperation to get away he enlisted for the US Army. Once inside he put in an immediate request to go to Afghanistan permanently. Her entire life she had been in and out of mental hospitals, trying various cocktails of medications, and moving state to state. Her mother Maxine enabled her and helped feed her delusions. Maxine had even gone as far as breaking Shondrella out of an institution. When Emory left and Shondrella got caught trying to burn down the command center at Fort Bragg, and that was the last straw. Maxine managed to get her out the hospital and away from the authorities and they went on the run. She told herself she was being a good mom by helping her daughter, but deep down inside she knew she was not helping.

She knew her daughter was not stable and needed help. At the very least she needed medications. It was difficult for Maxine to reprimand Shondrella because she was an only child and felt that her instability was due to being spoiled her entire life. Maxine was tired and running out of options, so she moved to South Carolina to get help from her brother Ralph.

Super excited, and already fantasizing about Donald, Shondrella rushed home to tell her mom the news about her boyfriend. "Mommy, Mommy, Mommy!" she was jumping up and down on the balls of her feet, "guess what happened to me today?" "What happened princess? Is everything alright?", Maxine asked with great caution. "Yes ma'am. Everything is perfect!", Clapping her hands together excitedly and smiling the biggest Kool-Aid smile she could smile she proceeded to tell her mom what happened that afternoon at the art gallery. "Uncle Ralph let me decorate his conference room, so I went to buy wall décor at the art gallery across the street. Her eyes started to space out as she continued. "I met him. The perfect man. I met my husband, Donald Murphy." Maxine tried to keep a straight face, but her heart was racing. This could not be happening again. "Tell me everything" was all she could manage to get out. Shondrella squealed, "He is tall, dark and handsome. Perfect white teeth. His voice is music to my ears. Skin like chocolate", she gushed. Maxine rolled her eyes, "I need you to stay focused, you said the same thing about the last ten men. Get your mind out of the gutter and stay focused girl". "Mommy this is different. I can feel it in my soul. I have to have this man." Shondrella sighed. "I'm in love". Maxine shook her head in disgust and exhaustion. "You have been doing so good off your medication, we don't need you having a setback. Don't start these fucked up delusions!" Shondrella scrunched up her face annoyed with her mom for not being on board with her plan. "MOMMY! He is mine you will see." Maxine was done. "You don't even know if he has a girlfriend or a wife. Hell for all you know he could be gay. I don't want you to get your hopes up."

Maxine turned to finish washing the dishes. "We just moved here and we're running out of states to run too. I can't have you fucking this up for us just because you think you are in love." "I know mommy. Besides, he must be single I did not see a ring on his finger, so I am claiming him" Shondrella kept raving on and on as she walked towards her room. "I refuse to move for you again Shondrella", Maxine called after her lovesick daughter. Ignoring her mother, Shondrella went to the bathroom to shower. She could not get Donald off her mind. She stepped into the steamy water and immediately began to play with her pussy. She imagined it was him washing her body and playing with her nipples. As she brought herself to an orgasm, she sighed to herself. "He has to be mine." Donald managed to put a tingle in her heart and between her thighs. Her love for him outweighed her feelings for any other man, even Emory. Unfortunately for Donald, Shondrella had never felt a love connection so strong and fast.

Chapter 2

BUT I LOVE HIM

MAXINE WAS HOPING THAT things did not get out of hand with this Donald situation, but she had a bad feeling. She knew how Shondrella got when faced with rejection, and she was not prepared to help her with any of her shenanigans this time around. In the past Maxine had helped her daughter do unspeakable things just to keep her happy, but not this time. She promised herself and her new man that she would not go back down that road again. Maxine was settling down nicely with a man, Ali Blackwell, who adored her and Shondrella. The two had been dating since she arrived in South Carolina, and Maxine was falling hard. Maxine decided she would live her life now, she refused to spend all her time catering to her daughter's tantrums. She begged her brother to help her. It was his idea to hire Shondrella at the law firm, to keep her busy and give her some normalcy. Shondrella did not need any free time. Who ever said that idle hands are the devil's playground, must have known Shondrella? This job helped everyone. It gave Shondrella a sense of direction and maturity. It allowed Ralph to help his family and get some much-needed help around the office. It gave Maxine a chance to rest and to function without being on the run. Maxine could not let this get crazy; she was just starting to live life.

Donald decided to surprise Courtney with a lunch date. He picked her up from work and they went to "Taste the Caribbean", a Jamaican restaurant just on the other side of Ralph's law firm and down the street from the art gallery. Donald pulled up to valet and opened the door for his woman. The two were walking and talking, totally engrossed in one another. Neither of them was paying attention and ran right into

Shondrella. She was there picking up lunch orders for the staff at the firm. Courtney apologized and proceeded to be seated.

Shondrella stood there dumbfounded, excited that she had just seen Donald but pissed because he did not even recognize her. Jealousy coursed through her as she watched Donald kiss Courtney and hold her hand. Shondrella left after five minutes or so, then she stormed out of the restaurant. She began gasping for air and holding her chest. She knew she had to hold it together before her family started to trip and send her away. Barely able to hold on to the bags of food, she delivered the food to everyone in the office and went to the backroom. She could not believe this was happening. She started rocking and scratching her arm. "he is mine" she repeated this a few times while digging into her arms causing them to bleed.

Shondrella was devastated and refused to lose her future husband before she had a chance to be with him.

Donald and Courtney sat in the back of the restaurant, in their own little world, staring lovingly at one another and talking. They shared their meals, the way lovers do and made conversation about the day. After paying and leaving the tip, Donald escorted his woman by hand to the car. Like any southern gentleman. "Thanks for lunch babe", Courtney said while kissing her love goodbye. "Anything for you Queen Bean", Donald laughed returning the kiss. The two shared a laugh at the nickname he had given her in college, because she survived mostly on Beanie Winnies. "Hey love, I have a few tattoo appointments at the Lily street shop tonight, so I won't be coming straight home", Donald reminded her of his schedule. He did not want her to worry about him or his whereabouts. "Ok baby call me later. Love you", Courtney called out while heading back into her building. She had the brightest smile on her face. She loved the fact that Donald dated her like he was still trying to get the goods. This made her want to give him everything he never knew he wanted and more.

Back at Ralph's firm, nobody realized that Shondrella was missing. She was grateful for that. She spent the rest of the day hiding herself and her panic attack in the back room. About thirty minutes before everyone was set to go home, she slid out the side door and rushed home. She had to come up with a plan to get her man. Donald made it to the shop early. He sat in the car reminiscing about when he first opened the doors. He had come a long way and would always remain humble to his craft and his beginnings. Donald had just finished setting up the studio for his client Frits. Frits was his roommate in college and a close friend. He had been waiting patiently for Donald's schedule to open so he could get in his chair. Everyone knew Donald was worth the time, money and energy for his ink work. "Wassup bro? How you been?", Donald greeted his friend with a brotherly hug. "Can't call it. Just minding my black owned business", Frits responded and handed Donald the drawing for the work he wanted done. "I feel you on that", Donald said motioning for him to have a seat in the chair while he put on his gloves. They chopped it up while Donald worked his magic. "I be seeing Alvin in the club all the time, that nigga stay turnt to the max", Frits laughed, "why don't you come with him sometimes". "Shiiiiitttt! Courtney aint having that man. She keeps me on the straight and narrow", Donald replied matter-of-factly. "Beside aint shit in these streets but death and a hard time. And I aint got time for that". Nodding in agreement, "Hell yeah. Nothing but loose pussy bitches and sack chasers out here. I am glad you and Courtney still kicking it. Thought you would have been married that girl". Laughing, "Very soon my nigga, Very soon. I'll go to war with God behind that one right there. That's wifey for sure", Donald declared. "I need me one of them kind in my life. You remember shorty I had?" Frits continued the small talk. "That trifling ass bitch was living a double life. She was married with kids. And had the nerve to stalk me and tear up my shit when I cut her ass off". They talked about their college days, and the raggedy bitches in the world, until the tattoo was finished. "Thanks man. I aint trust nobody else to do this here for me man", Frits said a little teary eyed. Donald just slayed a memorial tattoo for his mother. It was a picture of his mom wrapped in angel wings, floating in the clouds. She recently lost her battle with COPD and he was a momma's boy, so it was only right that he has her name on him. "This shit dope as fuck, I'm finna put this all across IG and Snap.", Frits said. "Fa Sho! And I sent your deposit back through cash app. I cannot charge you for this, she was another mother to me I still listen get lit off her favorite jam "BEFORE I LET GO". "Let's get up soon bro". They parted ways. When Donald finished with his last tattoo for the night, a simple 3D butterfly, he locked up and headed home. He was in his feelings after talking with Frits and decided he was going to hold Courtney a little tighter tonight. He knew how blessed he was to have found her so early in his life. He smiled at the thought of his baby sleep in bed and how he planned to wake her up when he got there.

Chapter 3

THE PERFECT FAMILY

THAT NIGHT WHEN DONALD made it in the house, he did exactly what he planned in his head. He kissed Courtney awake, and then made love to her. When they had finished, he held her close, and they talked. "Babe, how would you feel if I asked you to move in with me?" He asked. A half sleep Courtney replied, "is that even a question nigga, you know I'm with it". The next morning as they got dressed, Donald showed her the leaflet for a housing development. "I'm thinking this is a perfect place for OUR perfect family". Courtney could not stop smiling. It made sense that they live together. They slept together every night anyway, so one house versus two apartments was going to save money. They were comfortable sharing a living space, true partners in every sense. They decided on a house in Greenville. It was most practical, seeing as how one of the tattoo shops and the art gallery were all in Greenville. Courtney's job with DHSS had her between multiple job sites, so it did not matter for her.

Donald and Courtney decided to have a meet and greet to celebrate their progression in life together. They planned an evening with family and friends who would all be genuinely happy for them. They needed to know if the families would love each other as much as they did. Courtney had been around so long Vernetta, and Alvin already considered her family, but they families had extraordinarily little interaction so the two lovers wanted to see if they could be one big happy family. That was important for them both, especially Courtney. She would be heartbroken if they could not get along.

The night of the party everything and everyone were perfect. Ms. Vernetta and Alvin were introduced to all of Courtney's sisters and mom. It was an instant hit. They were all family and that was that. Courtney could not stop smiling, her heart was so happy. Vernetta and Sabrina sat down and was having a talk as though they were old friends. Sabrina, under the influence of wine, told the story of how Courtney became her daughter. "Honey, that's my child and God saw fit to send her my way, courtesy of my stupid ass ex best friend Marissa.", she said with tears in her eyes. "Marissa got caught up with this crazy ass man and after many outrageous incidents, he convinced her to leave town. What was supposed to be a weekend trip turned into weeks, months, and years. We have not heard from her since. As a best friend and mother, myself I could not let those girls go into the system, so I put my big girl panties on and the rest is history", Sabrina explained wiping her eyes. Vernetta admired her tenacity and authentic spirit. "A blessing in disguise, I'm sure. But how the hell you manage all girls? I always wanted one, but seven.", Vernetta laughed. "Mercy!" "Sabrina Wilks aint no punk bitch", Sabrina said, referring to herself in third person. "But honestly honey only the good lord brought me through that, cause seven attitudes, seven periods, seven personalities, Is a lot". The two laughed, before being interrupted and asked to rejoin the party.

Donald questioned his mom about her conversation with Ms. Sabrina. "Ma, what were you two over there plotting?". "Mind your business boy and give us a grandbaby", she responded with a laugh. She held her son's hand, "You have a special woman, a fragile woman, you take care of her son.", she advised. Donald just nodded in agreement. "That's my plan mom. I was raised by a beautiful woman, so I know perfection when I see it.", he complemented his mom. "Flattery will get you everywhere Donald Murphy", she laughed as they began mingling with everyone. The night was magical, and love was the theme for the evening.

"Wassup Big C", Courtney greeted her sister, and best friend. Big C hugged her "Hey gorgeous". The sisters began people watching and gossiping just like they did as kids. Pretty soon all the sisters were huddled together looking like a buffet of beauty. Seven different flavors of melanin magic. Any man with any sense noticed them and some women too. The girls were reminiscing about their childhood. They came a long way and most importantly, they came through together.

Courtney was one of seven. She was the oldest of her mother's children, followed by Zonjae (ZZ), and Cazandria (Caz). They are what people call stair steppers. Sabrina's four daughters were also stair step kids and roughly the same age, Big C is the oldest. Her real name is Chelsea, but her attitude was so big, and her body stature was so tiny, Big C was the only thing that seemed fitting for the 5'2 petite beauty. Bonnie, Dacemeber, named after her birth month and Beauty, named for her beauty mark on her cheek. The day that Sabrina officially took them in as her daughters they were, 15 (Big C), 14 (Bonnie), 13 (Courtney), ZZ and Dacember were both 12, Caz and Beauty are the babies. They were only 11. She smiled thinking of how Ms. Sabrina laid the law down to keep all of them in line. They turned out fine, but boy did they give her hell at times. Sabrina Wilks did not play, and she refused to let any of them go without anything or bully anyone. They did not tolerate disrespect. Not towards themselves, and definitely not towards one of their sisters. The motto Sabrina raised them on was "Family First", and "I am my sister's keeper". They got into so many fights in the neighborhood defending each other. Big C even ended up having to go to DJJ for six months. During her time away Courtney and Bonnie, took on the role of oldest and defender of all sisters. The girls were thick as thieves and that was the best thing. There was no need for friends because they had each other.

The sisters' trip down memory lane was interrupted when the DJ cut the music and Donald began talking. Everyone in attendance tuned in to see what he had to say. "Good evening everyone, I hope yall doing alright tonight.", he said as he moved to the front of the venue. "If any of you see my lovely lady in the crowd, can you send her my way. I need her for this". With no hesitation Courtney found her way to his side. Not missing a beat, he wrapped his arms around her shoulders and continued talking. "Yall, know we bet on yall tonight", he looked at a blushing Courtney. "I needed to know if our families could be a family, because I plan to make her my wife". The 'AWES' echoed through the room. "I know how important family is to this woman and I will move heaven and earth to make sure she has everything her heart desires. Family included.", flashing a smile at his mom who nodded to him in encouragement. Donald reached in his pockets and pulled out a key ring. "Courtney Mims, this morning I asked you if you were sure you wanted to move in and start a life with me, and you said yes. What you do not know is the house you think we are having built is already done. I wanted to surprise you." Holding the keys in her red face. "How did you manage that?" She questioned snatching the keys. "Easy, I asked for help. I relied on OUR sisters", and the two looked at the girls and smile. "Tell her what else we helped you with", Beauty yelled out, like to true brat she was. By the time Courtney turned back around she found Donald on bended knee holding a ring. "If you will allow me Ms. Mims, I would like to take this walk into forever with you as my wife, not my girlfriend". Standing ovation. "Bout damn time Donald", Courtney snatched to ring and put it on with a laugh. It was official. The meet and greet was the engagement party and the sisters knew everything. The rest of the night went without a problem. Nothing but good vibes, food, and fun everywhere.

Later that evening, when the two were getting ready for bed Courtney began asking questions. "Babe, what do you want, a summer or winter wedding?" Donald just gave her a look. "Don't look at me like that, this is your wedding too. I want you to have a say so in it." Donald climbed in the bed, taking the laptop from her and wrapping her in his arms. "Queen Bean, I want what you want. I want you to have the wedding of your dreams. No limits, No restrictions. Just you and your dreams, coming true. I want you. That is, it. Everything else is just icing on this cake", Donald said to her. "You know just what to say to get what you want huh", kissing him and sliding underneath his body, wrapping her legs around him, "So tell me what you want love. I am positive you already have it planned", Donald asked while leaving kisses down her collarbone and to her neck. "Don't laugh ok, but I want to get married on February 15th. Since It is the day after Valentine's day and the day before my birthday, it will give us a special 3-day celebration.". Donald stopped the kisses and just looked at Courtney. "You gonna make me work for the rest of my life I see.", he laughed. "Its just a childhood fantasy of mine. We don't have to do it if you don't want to", sounding disappointed that Donald didn't find the joy in her plans. Donald grabbed her face and kissed her passionately. "Are you talking about February 9 months from now or February a year and 9 months away?". She shrugged her shoulders. Kissing her again. "We will let 2022 be our anniversary, we have a clan of sisters and 2 overzealous mothers, I am sure they can get this thing done in 9 months. Besides, I have waited too long to make you mine anyway Mrs. Murphy". "Agreed, Mr. Murphy".

The two love birds started kissing and touching each other. Getting everything warmed up, Donald lifted her legs, getting ready to dive in between, but she stopped him with another question. "What about the place? The colors and décor? We have to answer these questions baby" "Courtney we will get all of that together, LATER". "Ok now when you end up wearing a pink velvet suit don't say nothing. Because imma tell everyone you did not care you was trying to be nasty.", she said with fake attitude. "The only pink I'm willing to wear is this pink pussy.", he said with a lick. "It can be on my face or on my dick. You choose. But that's all the pink for me" he said while licking her spot again. "Unless you trying to make this pink whipped cream disappear from my dick. Ill put pink on for you", he asked suggestively. "Oh, you aint said nothing but a word. You know I will always match your freak and your fly. Just tell me how you want it". Donald smiled, I know that's why you my wife. You are everything. Grabbing his dick and stroking it, I am your lover, friend, hoe, slut, anything else you think you need. I'm bout that life", She declared making his healthy 8 inched disappear into the back of her throat. The two spent the rest of the night and majority of the next morning making love and fucking. They spent hours making sure the other person was electrified and satisfied. When they were finally done and drifting off to sleep, Donald whispered into her ear, "You will be the mother of my children too". This was definitely a night to remember.

Chapter 4

SOMEBODY GET THIS GIRL

WHEN DONALD AND COURTNEY finally unwrapped themselves from one another it was the next day and time to get to work. "Wake up love. Its time to start the day." Donald kissed her awake. Smiling ear to ear and stretching she replied, "Do I have to?". "Of course not, you can always be a housewife and give daddy plenty of babies", Donald laughed as Courtney got up out of the bed. "I'd rather not daddy, there's so many kids out there depending on me, I can't sleep my life away". Courtney made her way to the bathroom but stumbled a little bit. "That's what good dick do to you", he said with a smug grin on his face. "Shut up nigga", she laughed as she pushed him. The two maneuvered around each other as they did hygiene and got dressed, sneaking kisses in every so often. They exited the house together and Donald helped Courtney to her car. "Have a good day Mrs. Murphy", he said with a kiss. "You too baby", she replied with a kiss of her own.

They parted ways and headed into work. Donald stopped at the art gallery first so he could catch up on some paperwork. He also had to inspect some wall art from France, which was already in the conference room waiting for him. While he was inspecting the new pieces, he took a conference call regarding the expansion and showcasing of his custom art pieces. He was determined to give his future family everything they never knew they wanted and then some. A true businessman through and through, he always gave 100%. He learned early on in business that the people working for him was just as important to be successful. He appointed his mom, Vernetta, as his assistant. Her office was at the gallery, but she managed the tattoo shops as well. Long ago he taught

Alvin how to tattoo and how to manage the shop. Alvin ran the shops and did ink work at his leisure, but he scheduled appointments for the other artists and Donald when he needed to. Alvin's focus was the ladies, and the clubs, so that was his budding business venture, but he was definitely going to help Donald keep his businesses running. Not only because that is his brother but because he knew that Donald will be helping him in any way possible. "All for one and One for all", they were the three musketeers, Him, Donald and their mom. This was Donald's team, and he knew he would not be anywhere without them.

Noticing that Donald had finally made it to work, Shondrella made her way over to the parking lot. Unnoticed, she placed a small tracking device on his car. Since her run in with him and Courtney at the restaurant she had been plotting on how to get next to him. She needed to know where he lived, she wanted to be able to keep tabs on him and know his every move. She did not see this as stalking, but more of making sure her man was ok. In her mind they were together and had a future. They were in love and just keeping things a secret for now. She had made love to him countless times over the weekend and he enjoyed it. At least that is what her mind was telling her. After attaching the GPS to his car, Shondrella walked into the gallery, bold as ever, "May I speak with the owner?". Vernetta looked at her sideways but responded professionally, "The owner is busy at the moment, but I will be happy to have a specialist help you". Shondrella blew out an aggravated breath, "No! It must be the owner. I'm surprising him with a lunch date today", adjusting her dress. "He is my boyfriend". Vernetta held it together, but barely because she knew damn well this little girl was not about to mess up Donald's life with Courtney. With a pointed look, "Honey, its cute that you have a crush on my son", stressing the son part. "But I can assure you that whatever you think you have with him is a whole lie, He is happily engaged to his long-time girlfriend". "Where is my man? You need to go and get him before I get upset!", Shondrella demanded. "He told me to meet him here", she started to yell. Before Shondrella could protest, Vernetta said, "I do not know who in the fuck raised you, but I am about to have you rapping with 2-pac if you don't bring that shit down". "My son doesn't have time for the bullshit, and I don't tolerate fuckery". "So would you like some assistance buying artwork or do you need assistance exiting the building". "Both are just a phone call away love". Vernetta was as sweet as they came until you messed with one of her kids, that she did not play about. Buckeye overheard the commotion and came to see what was going on. Immediately, he grabbed Shondrella, "Ma'am it is time for you to go. Please and Thank you", as he forcibly escorted her from the building.

Ralph was on his way back into the office for a meeting with a client when he notices all the commotion. When he took a closer look, he could see Shondrella being forcefully removed from the art gallery. He immediately went to intervene and see what the problem was. Buckeye explained the entire situation. Shondrella tried to deny everything saying she was being manhandled and touched inappropriately. "Sir, I assure you that is not the case, and you are welcome to view our security cameras", Buckeye told Ralph. "That will not be necessary, all I ask is that you not press charges. Please allow me to deal with my niece as this is a family matter", Ralph went on to explain Shondrella's condition and how unstable she was. He offered to pay for any damages and promised to keep her from causing any more problems. Vernetta and Buckeye agreed to let her go with her uncle but told him if she caused any more problems the police would have to get involved. Grabbing Shondrella by the arm, Ralph walked her across the street calling his sister at the same time. He was pissed to say the least, "Here we go again". Ralph demanded that Maxine come down to the office so he could fill her in on the fuckery her daughter already found herself in. Monica, Ralph's wife, told him to send them away or at least have Shondrella committed because this was an on going and growing problem. "You're enabling both of them baby, this won't end well", she yelled and stormed out of his office just as Maxine walked in. "Good afternoon sis, I wont beat around the bush. Shondrella is on her bullshit again and needs her meds ASAPLY!! Because what I will not do is be embarrassed or charged with crimes for helping her crazy ass.", Ralph went in instantly. "What the hell happened?" was the only thing Maxine asked? She knew it was something crazy, but she needed all the details. She was hoping that there was a reasonable explanation for it all but by the time Ralph finished the story all she could do was shake her head. "Young lady why in the hell are you disturbing those people at the art gallery?" she asked her daughter. With a roll of her eyes, Shondrella answered, "All I wanted was to see my man, damn". "He is not your man!" Maxine exclaimed. "You don't know him from a fart in the wind and you wanna run behind him.

You will sit your hot ass down and act like you have some sense. I refuse to do this shit with you again. This fetish for a man has gone on long enough and cost us too much for me to continue playing into your fantasies. Do you understand?" Shondrella just sat there quiet trying to find her words. "Ralph I'm so sorry. I need another favor. Can you get me a supply of medications?", handing her brother the laundry list of medicines that Shondrella needed. "I will not risk everyone's life on her mental stability. We have been running state to state hiding and surviving. I'm ready to live." Maxine continued to rant. "NO MOMMY PLEASE! I do not need those pills I swear". "I will do better I won't cause any problems for anyone," Shondrella cried. "Apparently you do need them, and you will have them, and you will take them even if I have to shove them down your throat my damn self". "I went out on a limb and did all kind of illegal shit just to get you and your mom here and you risk it all for a whimsical crush". "NO MA'AM." Ralph's voice boomed. Shondrella and Maxine flinched. "The meds make me sleep all day and feel funny". "I don't like them", she begged with tears in her eyes. "I personally don't give a rats ass if they make you fly, you better take them". Ralph was so serious. Maxine was teary but remained strong. "Its for all of our sake. You will take them and that is that. "I am finally happy for the first time in God knows how long. You will not ruin that. Now here take the damn pills", Maxine handed her a cocktail of medications. With a wet face Shondrella took the meds and sat on the couch as instructed. Buckeye was told to keep an eye on her until Maxine was ready to go. The siblings went to his office to discuss how they would be handling Shondrella from here on out and how they would keep her supplied with meds. Getting the meds were the easy part. Ralph did great work and knew lots of people in high places. Those people would give him anything because he kept them and their children out of jail. Thirty minutes later Ali, Maxine's boyfriend arrived, and they left as a family.

Once they left Monica had her own words for her husband. She was not a fan of Maxine or Shondrella and thought about turning them in daily. Only thing really stopping her was the fact that Ralph would get caught up in all of that and she would protect her man at all costs. "What the fuck them bitches need now Ralph?", Monica said full of hatred while giving him the side eye. Ralph sat down on the floor laying his head in her lap and proceeded to tell her about everything. Monica listened and gave her take on things as needed while massaging his scalp. She was his rider for sure, but he needed to get off this ride because she was not happy at all.

When Maxine finally got Shondrella in her bed and set up the cameras, she broke down and told Ali everything. "Baby I understand how wrong I was, and I know I should have been firmer and gotten her more help, but I felt like I was abandoning her, and I just couldn't. And now I am here and in love with you and she is starting up again. I don't have it in me to go on the run again." Ali just listened and held her close. When she was done talking, he told her that he understood her reasons, "Baby in order to get different you have to do different. I love you and I am here to help you both, but we are not helping her with her crazy. You must put your foot down. I will support you through this all but don't keep anything from me.". Ali held on to his woman while she cried for the rest of the night. He felt confident that they would get through this and that with medication Shondrella could be controlled.

Chapter 5

NO MORE EXCUSES

Aᴛᴇʀ Fɪɴɪsʜɪɴɢ Uᴘ Wɪᴛʜ a conference call and some other business, Donald walked out of his office to find his mother. He was going to ask her if she wanted to go to lunch but instead was bombarded with a recount of what had just happened. Donald was shocked to say the least. He had no clue who this mystery lady could be, and he wanted to know who could be that crazy to disrupt a business on a prank. Looking back at the footage he noticed the female from the other day that was purchasing art for the law firm across the street. His eyebrows were furrowed together as he shit to himself about all the bullshit he and his brother got into back in the day. He wondered if this was his past coming back to bite him in the ass. He had his fair share of broken hearts and he knew just how crazy a woman could get. This was different though; the entire situation was simply crazy as hell. "The uncle said that she is very much off her rocker and that he would make sure she doesn't come back around us making any problems.", Vernetta assured her son. She saw the wheels in his head turning. "Ok, lets stay on top of this thou. I can't have this killing my business.", he said exasperated. Still unable to make it make sense, Donald called it a day and went home to find Courtney there. She greeted him with a kiss, and he started to tell her about the incident at the gallery. "AWWWW! My boo got a secret admirer", she said jokingly. She helped him realize that this young lady really might have a mental disorder and not to read so much into it. It was not personal. "I hope you are right", he said as he helped her prepare dinner for the night.

21

Shondrella was sound asleep. Maxine made sure of it by checking on her constantly and keeping the time schedule for her meds consistent. She and Ali took turns checking the home cameras and checking the in-house alarms. They were trying to anticipate anything Shondrella could think to do and stop it before it got out of hand. Maxine knew firsthand how sneaky and conniving Shondrella could be, and she was not having it. She knew her daughter would try something she just did not know when. Two weeks had past, and everything was going well for everyone. Shondrella had been properly and heavily medicated, Maxine and Ali were head over heels for each other, and Donald had managed to forget about the incident and focus on the surprise birthday party he was planning for Courtney. He decided to leave all the wedding planning to the women. Courtney was able to get Zen Fuller to plan the wedding. She saw her work on IG and Facebook and had to have her. Zen Fuller was insta-famous, and her work spoke VOLUMES. It was a miracle and a pretty penny, but she had an opening and Courtney jumped on it. She has been over the moon about being able to work with her. The two meets at least once a week to combine and discuss the wedding. Her sisters and the mothers were all on board too. Ms. Vernetta had her own party planning and decorating business, so this was up her ally. Especially since she only had sons, so she was never given the opportunity to be extra girly about anything. So that left Donald to do as he pleased. He found a nice all-inclusive 5-star hotel that would be the venue. He had blocked off 2 of the 5 floors for the guests and since it was a three-day celebration, he planned to have her a surprise birthday party amid all the chaos that was wedding planning.

As far as he knew the colors were pink, purple, and grey. He knew that everything would be extravagant and decorated down to the silverware. So, he planned to piggyback off the wedding and reception making her birthday all pink with splashes of purple and grey. He had spoken with Zen privately, and communicates with her only through email, but she helped him order the special pieces that would make the room romantic and special. His goal was to make all his wife's to be dreams come true. Everything was going well, and everyone was all smiles. Life was good. Nobody was aware that Shondrella was still obsessing over her love and infatuation with Donald, and she had a plan that was getting ready to fuck everything up.

Shondrella managed to start throwing up her meds. Maxine made sure she swallowed them, so she had become good at throwing them up shortly after her mom left the room. So, no one knew but Shondrella was unmedicated and determined more than ever. She needed to get out of the house and to get rid of Courtney. Her jealous spirit would not allow her to see anything but red when Courtney was concerned. In her mind, Courtney was messing with her man and she was not going to have that. She was like a poisonous snake waiting to strike. It was 2am when she got her chance, she overheard Maxine and Ali having sex, she used that as her opportunity to leave. Placing some things in her backpack the GPS tracker being one. She tipped toed to the door but spotted the inside alarm the lights were flashing green, and the door had multiple locks. She went to the window and raised it up softly she held her breath and took a leap into the bushes on the side of the house. She had no clue where she was going. Two hours had passed by, she end up in an all-night coffee shop. She was wired up off coffee still contemplating on how she can get Donald. It was 6am time for Shondrella's first daily dose of medication. Maxine enters the room still half sleep with a glass of water in one hand and a medication cup in the other. Maxine bends down to tap Shondrella to see her bed was empty, she let out a painful from the gut scream. Ali comes running with his Glock ready for war, "she gone is all Maxine could say repeatedly". "Calm down let's take a look at the camera said Ali". Maxine starts to get dress feeling like a nervous wreck, she paced back and forth until Ali called her close to the camera telling her to look. The two spent hours going over the footage of the last few days. They discover how she made her get away and seen her making herself vomit up her medication. "I let my guard down and that heifer outsmarted me; we got to find her ASAP Maxine said loud and angry. Maxine and Ali left the house in search of Shondrella. Maxine decide not to tell Ralph just yet, it was now 5pm they deiced to get a bite to eat while they figure out a plan to find Shondrella. They enter the Waffle house and soon as they were seated Ali grabbed Maxine hands "we going to find her, but you are going to have to part ways with her she's ill ". You have been going through this for years the situation is getting worse let me help you, stop being her crutch and be her mom you deserve happiness I love you, so let me love you and don't push me away". Ali poured his heart out to Maxine, she responded, "I know what I got to do now she must be committed no more excuses".

Chapter 6

THIS IS BULL-SHIT

AFTER SHE DRIED HER eyes and laid under Ali for a little while longer, Maxine did what she had to do. She called Ralph, to give him the news. She did not want to, but she had no choice. Maxine needed his help. They had to find Shondrella and fast. "What the fuck Maxine?", Ralph yelled, "How could you let this happen? I thought you said you had it under control!" Monica just sat and watch her husband yell and raise his blood pressure. She was livid. Her hatred for Maxine and Shondrella grew every time their messy asses needed something. "Alright man, Damn. Just be at the office as soon as possible. We got to figure this shit out". Slamming the phone down, Ralph screamed out in frustration. Monica just shook her head, "What now Ralph? What them bitches need now?". "Nothing man, I can handle it", he said, not wanting to hear his wife's mouth. No such luck though because Monica refused to be uncomfortable or be quiet. Anything pertaining to Maxine and Shondrella made her ass itch. "When is all of this madness going to stop", Monica was off the couch and in his face in a flash. "This is going to get worse especially if you keep helping them.". Standing in front of the door pleading with her eyes, "Leave it alone baby, you can't keep jumping in and saving the day". "They are some ungrateful selfish ass trolls, and you will go crazy as them trying to help them." Ralph leaned down and kissed the top of his wife's head, "Not now baby, Its family. I have to help them". "You keep on putting out their fires and watch how you end up burned, she folded her arms and watched her husband leave to go save the day.

When Ralph arrived, Ali nor Maxine could read his face. He was in lawyer mode, complete with the poker face. Maxine started to speak but he raised his hand to silence her. "I will be your attorney because they will more than likely bring charges against you for helping Shondrella escape and flee.", Ralph stated matter of fact, giving the meat and potatoes of the situation at hand. "The way I see it you are facing, a laundry list of charges and most of them are felonies. But I'm sure you didn't think of any of that while you were helping her.". Ralph's voice was serious but light. You could tell he was fed up with all of this. "This can and probably will get ugly but first things first. We have to find Shondrella". The rest of the meeting was spent with Ralph calling in favors to his people, on both sides of the law. He put the word out on the street, "Bring her to me safely, unharmed, no police, and you get half a mill". Ralph was no stranger to the street code, so he knew that money talked. "We need to go inform these people that your daughter is going to be coming for them, help them the best we can to prepare and deal with this shit storm. Hopefully, they will not be too harsh when this is all over", he said standing up and buttoning his jacket. The three walked across the street together. The look of reluctance on Maxine's face was so obvious, but Ralph did not give two fucks.

"Good day is Mr. Donald Murphy in?", Ralph asked Buck-eye. "Can you please let him know this is an urgent matter?". Buck-eye did as asked, and called Donald to the conference room for the meeting. When Donald walked up Ralph extended his hand, then Ali. Once all the pleasantries were out of the way, "How can I help you all?", Donald asked. Diving right into the issue at hand, Ralph told Donald all about Shondrella and her obsession with him. He explained that her mental diagnosis caused her to act out her delusions. "I have never done anything to give her that impression, I thought I made it clear when she came over the last time that there was nothing between us." Donald was totally confused and in disbelief. "Unfortunately, you did not need to do anything, Shondrella has formed this unhealthy attachment to you. "We are trying everything in our power to get her back home safely so that she can receive the help she needs". I just felt it was necessary to give you a heads up about what is going on, especially since she will more than likely show herself to you sooner rather than later." Ralph said. Maxine stayed quiet. She knew her brother was doing the right thing, but it hurt her heart to hear them discuss Shondrella like she was nothing. After an hour or so, Donald is dumb struck, but he finds his voice. "This shit is crazy, and I appreciate the heads up, but please understand; I will protect my family at all costs". I don't wish any harm to her, nor do I plan to hurt her, but if push comes to shove and shove push back", Donald shrugged his shoulders to say, "it is what it is". "Respectfully", the men shook hands again. Ralph handed Donald his card, "Here is my personal number, please feel free to call me at any time". Donald gave him his information as well. "I will definitely keep you posted on everything".

The next stop was the local police station. Maxine really did not want to file a missing person's report, but Ralph was on her ass. "The public needs to know about this incase she is spotted", I have my people on it, they are working overtime to get her found. Maxine gave the report she carefully left out the part about Shondrella's previous escapes, as instructed by Ralph. He also helped her pick out the most innocent looking picture to give to the press. The people needed to see her without malice. "We will get this information out to the news outlets as soon as possible. It will run in the morning paper as well." A desk officer explained to them.

They rode back to the office in silence. Ralph pulled up beside Ali's car and put the car park. "ENOUGH IS ENOUGH! And I am speaking as your brother not your lawyer." Shondrella needs the kind of help and attention that you cannot provide". When she is apprehended this time, she will be taken into custody and that is where she will stay" Ralph spoke slowly and deadly. "I know Ralph.", she started but he cut her off. "Maxine I'm not fucking around with you, you cut her off or I cut you off. End of story." Hitting the unlock button for them to exit. He barely waited for them to close his door all the way before pulling off. He drove straight home to his wife. He knew that running to the rescue of his sister and niece all the time put a strain on his marriage. He was trying to figure out what he could do to make it up to Monica, because through it all she always held him down. She was surly the Bonnie to his Clyde. When he walked in the house, Monica was sipping on her favorite cocktail, Stella Rose Peach and Peach Crown, and listening to old school R&B. She was clearly still very pissed about earlier and rightfully so. He kissed the top of her head; no words were spoken. He took his clothes off preparing for a shower. Monica Breaking the silence, "When are you going to stop this shit? Huh. "You are about to find yourself in a lot of bullshit following them up, and please know that you will be in it alone because I refuse to be your co-defendant because of your sick and twisted family". "I know you love them, and they are family but so am I", I am the one that has to see your heart break when they don't even speak to you unless their hands are out, begging like the bums they are". "You don't even get a birthday card or a Christmas card, how grimy is that"? But you run to their every beck and call, those two shysters are playing you like a puppet". Monica had started crying. Ralph hugged her tight. "Baby I know. Everything you are saying is true and I cannot do this or anything without you. All of the sweet things you do and how you love me extra hard does not go unnoticed". I will be better; I will do better I promise". "I need you baby, Ralph steps up close to Monica; "show me some love", he then pucker up his lips. Monica kissed her husband with all the love and desperation she felt. "We will see love", patting his chest and leaving him to take his shower.

Chapter 7

JUST SALVAGE

THREE WEEKS HAS PASSED and not a word or visual of Shondrella. Shondrella had found a house two streets over from Donald and Courtney, she had been sleeping in a RV parked neatly in this yard. The RV was packed with all the essentials she needed to survive. There were three beds and a working bathroom. She later found a remote that lead her to a lower area that was just as stocked and nice. Apparently, this household is about to take a trip. Beach balls, swimsuits, beach towels, sunscreen the set-up screams family vacation. The house belonged to the John and Lizzie Dunlap. They had twin boys Leon and Leroy age 23, and a daughter Magic 21. Magic had a 3-year-old daughter named Love. The family were going to be headed out to Florida in a few days for their annual summer vacation. Shondrella had discovered a pathway that gave her a clean view of Donald's and Courtney house. She would sneak out and look for hours sometimes she would see Donald leaving. She then would go back in the RV and pleasure herself by masturbating. This is something she did often since grade school. Shondrella would have conversations with the thin air as if she were talking to Donald. She even responded taking over the role of him saying to herself how much he loves her. Now the type of delusional disease Shondrella has, she will believe this event is actually taking place. She is off her medication, so her mind is free game to go hay wire. The twins Leroy and Leon along with a friend of theirs Chuck they went to the RV to smoke a blunt. The guys begin to roll up, they were scrolling through their phones checking the hype on social media. It was several minutes before they heard sex sounds coming from the lower deck. Shondrella was playing in her pussy having a full sex encounter by herself but in her mind Donald was there. Leon was the first to say, "y'all niggas here that"? "I thought I heard something", said Chuck. Leon said its coming from below", Leroy said I'm going to get dad". "nigga sit your scary ass down". They open the door and the noise got louder; they begin to slow creep down the small number of steps. Leon being the first to see Shondrella digging her pussy out. Chuck and Leroy focused in on the action as well. "If I had a condom, I would fuck this bitch said Chuck". "Who is this he then asked"? The twins both replied, "I do not know". Like the young niggas they were they continued to watch and enjoy the show she put on, she starts to get weird by talking to the imaginary Donald. Shondrella yells out fuck me harder Donald, yes daddy give me that dick". Shondrella was convinced she was getting fucked. Leroy says, "we must get this lady out of here she does not belong in our RV this is strange". Chuck said, "I agree". "Shit like this don't happen in our neighborhood said Leroy". Leon dropped his phone, Shondrella heard the noise then jumps up she grab her clothes and starts to put them back on. "Leon asked "who the fuck is you and why are you in our family RV"? "I'm Shondrella some men are after me, their trying to kill me". "I been running for two day I found this spot last night; the door was open so; I just came in to hide out". Sex eases my mind that is why I had to get my rock soft". "I hope you fellas don't make me leave. I'll do anything I have no one ". "This is my mom and dad's establishment we have no control over that said Leon, I'll bet my right arm mom is going to flip out if not call the police". "The best thing for you to do ma'am is just leave". Leon starts to get aggravated because the more the guys tried to get her out of the RV and get her to kick rocks, the more comfortable she became. "Look bitch we have been too damn nice considering that you are trespassing and breaking the damn law, you got to get the fuck out of here". "So, walk your horny ass back to the top and leave". Chuck said firmly". I really need you guys to help me, please do not call the police or alert your parents". "We do not know you; how the fuck we suppose to collaborate with a fucking psycho, because clearly that's what you are". Leroy said while hoping she just leave. Shondrella ran up top grabbed her backpack seconds later the guys were right behind her. She took out a fake grenade, anyone one the opposite end could not tell it was a fake it was a complete replica.

"Shondrella held up the grenade and said, "I am not psycho you need to apologize to me right mutha fuckan now before I pull this pin and we all blow up in this bitch". "Leroy threw his hands up in surrender mode he then begins to apologize singing it loud and begging like Keith Sweat for her to calm down. "Now that I got y'all undivided attention this is what's about to go down". "You boys are going to help me rather you like it or not, because the grenade will blow up this whole entire street if you feel like doing otherwise". "Our parents got money let us go we can get you what you want; no need to hurt us we done nothing to you a crying Leroy pleaded". "What do you want from us said Chuck"? "I know by now I have made the news so pull your phones out and check my status, I have escaped from several mental institutions and I'm off my medication which causes me to make unjudgmental decisions". "I'm a delusional wreck and very unstable", life dealt me a lunatic hand that keeps me going haywire". "So, my advice to you is do not try me or we all die". "So, you really going to make my family suffer from your short comings, bitch you need a mutha fukan doctor you passed delusional, you fukan nuts Leon spoke". Leon has in his head that the three of them being men they can take her regardless of that grenade, he was thinking they at least had to try this bitch and take control over the situation. "Leon was trying to talk to Chuck with his eyes and body language. All he could come up with is they could rush her, so he continued to look at his phone reading the news write up about her. Why he placed a quick text to Chuck saying, "when I blink hard rush her ass". Leroy should automatically join in. Shondrella begin to talk about moving in the house, Leon blinks hard and he and Chuck rushed her they bumped heads with each other at first but quickly recovered, just as planed Leroy joined in, they got her down and begin to beat on her trying hard to knock her out. Chuck manages to get the grenade and went outside to lay it on the sidewalk they did not let up on her. Dragging her out the RV bumping her head along the way once outside Chuck start to kick her, Leroy said "hold up this is a female we can't overpower her like this". "Nigga this bitch was about to pull the plug on our ass seconds ago fuck this bitch Leon screamed". "You right bro", they kept the kicks coming. Magic looks out the window and see the commotion she comes out with a bat asking her brothers what the fuck is going on, Leroy turns around and say go get mom and dad and call the police this bitch tried to kill us". The police came and Shondrella was arrested, they found out from the bomb squad that the grenade was a fake. The police congratulated the guys and gave them a number to claim the big reward. The parents were in shock that something like this happen in their yard after they been there over 30 years.

Chapter 8

THE GET AWAY

SHONDRELLA WAS TAKEN TO the Greenville County Detention center and booked on escape and kidnapping charges. After she sees the judge in the am she will go to the maximum-security mental health jail in Spartanburg. Her Family was notified of her capture and they felt so much relief. Maxine refused to go see her she would wait until she went back on her medication. Donald and Courtney were informed that Shondrella was in custody. Courtney was happy because she thought her, and her sisters were about to get some wreck and hurt this chick. Not to mention what the fuck Sabrina would do; her mom was hood crazy. Sabrina was a OG certified gangster. Courtney still thinks the whole situation was weird. This type of shit happens on lifetime movies. Courtney and the sisters got together with the wedding planner and came up with the hair styles down to the footwear. Maxine and Ali had decided to take things up a notch and get married. They had a small ceremony with 10 guests at Ralph's estate. Monica was away on a business trip, so Ralph was able to extend his hospitality. Days after the wedding Ali took Maxine on a cruise to relax her mind and get away from all the Shondrella mess. Maxine seemed to be distant and worried, he also noticed her twitching and biting her nails, he did not think much of it at the time. Ali had to put her in check by telling her to snap out of it, he gave her a motivational speech about her own happiness. Shondrella had been moved to the mental facility she was already looking for ways to escape. She had been managing to cheek her medication and stashing the pills in between her butt cheeks, she was giving a small flimsy toothbrush that bent back with ease. She had started a sharping process on the toothbrush hiding it in the same place as the pills. The guard's question her about the toothbrush because she was supposed to turn it in. She told the guard that another guard had taken it, it was believable because sometimes that does happen. Shondrella had a male roommate he was so medicated all he did was sleep. Shondrella had a plan that was going to satisfy her and get her a co-defendant. Shondrella was waiting on lights out, and for the guards to do their hourly rounds. She then creeps over to the mans bed side she lifted his gown and starts to rub on his dick. She massages his dick slowly and he begin to rise. She placed her mouth and proceeded with oral sex, she massages his genitals and placed them in her mouth as well. After minutes of slurping and moaning she then gets on top of him placing his dick inside of her vagina she grinds on him hard and fast pleasuring herself. Shondrella heard some keys so she jumps up quickly and gets back in her bed, she pulled the cover over her head and remained still as possible. The guard shines his flashlight and all he seen was Clifton's dick sticking straight up in the air. He thought to himself, what a dream. Weeks passed by and Shondrella had gained the trust of a night guard Ms. Margret, she would let Shondrella give her roommate Clifton his medication so she would not have to go inside the room. Shondrella did not give him his medication she stashed it with the others. She continued the sex acts with Clifton only now he was alert and enjoying it, she blew his mind night after night. Clifton had never had sex before he has been institutionalized since grade school. He often played with it every chance he got but he stayed medicated it was not often. Like every man he likes the feeling of warm pussy, blind cripple or crazy sex is sex. He enjoyed being touched by Shondrella it gave him a mushy love feeling on the inside, that he grew fond of. Shondrella went over an escape plan with Clifton and promised she would sex him up on the regular if he helped her get out. Clifton was all smiles and would kill at this moment if she asked. Ms. Margret came around to do her rounds and Shondrella was lying in bed while Clifton was bent over naked in a pile of vomit, Ms. Margret automatically went into save mode and opened the unit gate. She rushes over to Clifton to see what was wrong. Clifton immediately stabbed her with the toothbrush Shondrella makes her move and took his grown and gaged her mouth. She then took a needle off the med cart placing the pills that she smashed up earlier mixed them with some saline then place the concoction inside the needle. she sticks her with the needle and place her in the bed. Shondrella grabs Ms. Margret keys then grabs on to Clifton's hand. After closing the door and they ran down the hall into the first utility closet they see. Shondrella looks around for a uniform or any type of clothing. Clifton just looked around dumbfounded waiting on his next command from Shondrella. Stanley the janitor had a cleanup in the staff restroom he heads for the utility closet to get what he needed. As Stanley opens the door the two hid behind a shelf. Shondrella opens a bottle of bleach along with some other chemicals from the shelf, she gives Clifton a nod once the opportunity presented itself Shondrella rushes over to Stanley grabbed him by the neck and begin to pour the bleach down his face she opens his mouth so the bleach can make it down his throat, Clifton followed her lead doing the other cleaning chemicals the same way. Stanley could not put up a fight he started to shake. After a few minutes, the bottles were empty Shondrella took off his uniform covered in chemicals, she placed them on herself. Shondrella spots a laundry basket then instructs Clifton to climb inside. She was now in Stanley's full uniform even the steal toe boots. She rolls the basket out of the closet and begin to find the exit. Breathing hard but trying to relax Shondrella was pushing the basket at a fast pace, she spots an exit, and her breathing begins to slow down. She was quick on her feet when she took Stanley's swipe key Shondrella approaches the exit door and swipe the key, the door pops open she holds her breath while she walks to another door luckily, she swipes the key, and that door opens too. Roger another janitor yells out Stanley you still need to clean up the staff room, Shondrella turn around and looks down and nods her head giving him a thumbs up. She now was more than halfway out she just had to get through the main gate. She reaches the gate, and the gate requires a code to get out she screams fuck and begin to panic Clifton peeps up and starts to stutter trying to say what is wrong. She whispers" we need a fucking code to get out", "dammit were fucked". Clifton repeated 1111, Shondrella ignoring him trying other numbers Clifton yells out 1111 bitch. Shondrella put that code in, and the gate pops open she push through the gate not bothering to close it back. She speeds walks to the parking lot to find Ms. Margret's car. She hits the alarm when it sounded off, she followed the sound, once they made it to the car a still naked Clifton gets in the back and lay down while Shondrella crank the car and pulls off full speed. Clifton knew the code from leaving out with the guards a few times for a doctor visits, the guards would often say the code aloud; they never thought he would ever get to use it.

Chapter 9

NOT AGAIN

SHONDRELLA AND CLIFTON MANAGED to make their way to Greenville. Their first stop was a laundry mat, they stole some clothes and shoes out of the dryers. Shondrella parks the car in the hospital garage, hoping to find another car to steal but no one was dumb enough to leave their keys in the car. Bad as she hated to walk it was best, the car as about to be on the radar by the police. Back at the mental facility Ms. Margret had been found she was not hurt bad, her thick uniform saved her. She just played like she was out of it so he would stop sticking her and think she was dead. She will be given some drugs to counter act the medications Shondrella had stuck her with. Stanley was in ICU he had damage to his lungs and had consumed lots of toxins from the chemicals his throat had closed, and his skin was bruised badly. An emergency alert was in place the police and FBI were out looking for two escapees, roadblocks were set up, Shondrella's and Clifton's pictures was plastered all over the news. Before the facility could call the families, Ralph had seen the news and noticed his niece picture, he slammed his hand on the coffee table and broke it in half. "Monica was calling his phone he already knew she had seen the news; Ralph did not answer her would deal with his wife later he had bigger fish to fry. Ralph grabs his phone and calls Maxine; she answers all happy what's up bro you want to get some dinner Ali will be working late and I'm hungry"? "Shondrella escaped Ralph said in a low tone, Maxine smile turned into a frown she begins to shake. "What the fuck you mean escaped"? "This can't be that is a high maximum facility". "It's all over the news check it out sis; I'm on my way to pick you up we are going to that facility to get some fuckan answers". Ralph picks up Maxine they talk the entire 45-minute drive about the escape. They reach the facility; they both jump out the car like the government was giving out free stimulus checks. Ralph reaches the front desk and yells out "I need to see whomever is in charge". The lady at the desk who name tag read Tonya says" sir how can I help you I'm the lead staff on the shift". "No disrespect ma'am I need to see the director the chief of staff there is nothing you can do for me at this time". "I'll call someone right away sir". Ralph starts talking out loud while waiting on someone of management to approach him, Ralph was past aggravated. A tall slender man walks up to them and says, "hello I'm Conrow Evens, you seem to have a problem sir". "Fuck yeah I got a problem how the hell this facility let my niece who is a habitual offender of escapes, escape again". "sir we are working around the clock to fix this, I just fired several staff for sleeping and being slack on the job". "I totally understand your frustration I have all my veteran staff on duty striving hard for the capture of your niece and the other escapee". Trust me we will find them, were calling all cars I assure you". Maxine spoke up "sir please look at my daughters file she is a nut case". "This is not her first rodeo she can be dangerous when things don't go her way, or she don't get what she wants; you must find her". Yes, ma'am I apologize my facility takes full responsibility for this mishap, I must go I have to direct the search party I'll keep you posted here is my card call me anytime". Maxine suggested they warn Donald and his family once again, Ralph agreed. On the ride back Maxine calls Donald and she gives him the run down on the situation at hand. The call was brief and to the point, after Donald disconnected from Maxine, he goes and finds his fiancé Courtney who was getting ready for a court case. "Bae you know I just got a call from that crazy ass girl moms the crazy bitch has escaped from the mental institution in Spartanburg, they think she on her way to find us". "I just seen that on the news I wouldn't have never thought it was her, I'm getting tired of this nut bucket looney toon ass freak". "Just be careful leaving out and pay attention to your surroundings, this bitch definitely has a problem". "I have our surveillance camera on, plus I called BG he's going to ride around and case the block for anything suspicious". BG was Donald's younger cousin he is known for riding around smoking his weed with his friends all day, so Donald gave him a job. The community pay him to do security patrol, he has caught a lot of burglars and peeping toms in the area. If anybody is lurking the community BG and his crew will spot them, they do their best work high.

Chapter 10

Playing Hide And Seek

SHONDRELLA AND CLIFTON END up at the Dunlap household.[i] Shondrella knew they were gone out of town from her previous experience with them. They camped outside of the house for hours trying to find a way in. Shondrella finds the power box and cut the power off she breaks a window, and they climb inside. With the power off the alarm will not go off. Clifton starts to ramble through the kitchen and finds a few flashlights, they look through the entire home and find all kind of gadgets. Making their self at home eating and drinking on wine, they had candles burning and found batteries for a clock radio that was in one of the twin's room. Shondrella asked Clifton did he know how to eat pussy, He said "I have seen it done on a DVD movie one of my roommates had in my old placement". "it can't be that hard it looks fun"." Come over here and let me see how much you know". Clifton moves closer and bend down looking nervous Shondrella legs were already open she had already start to pleasure herself with her hand, Clifton immediately dives in. Little did Shondrella know his pussy licking skills were on point, he latched on that pussy sucking and pulling hard but gentle. He was licking her up and down from the front to the back, he then starts to tongue fuck her she was going out her mind and having countless orgasms. Clifton had to have been study the hell out of them DVD movies because he was in beast mode. Shondrella was rocking and rotating her hips, she palmed his head with a death grip Clifton could not move, it was like he was under water gasping for air. Shondrella had in her mind that Donald was the one pleasuring her she smiled and did not want the feeling to end. After two hours of spectacular head from Clifton, she wanted more. Clifton could not come up for air, Clifton became her in house sex slave she was taking full advantage of him. He finally switched the lineup and turned her over and put his dick in her mouth, he was slow but not that slow. Shodrella was on cloud 9 with Donald face glued to her peripheral vision, she sucked him off good and then turned around and let him ass fuck her Clifton was going ham pounding hard in her ass. He was fucking her like a zoo animal, he put all his strength into action. Clifton not knowing what an orgasm felt like he was screaming bloody murder, shaking profusely when he nutted, he was so loud you would have thought he was getting his ass kicked instead of bussin a nut. Clifton never felt so good in his life. He was pussy whipped from that moment on. They fell asleep and did not wake up until morning. Waking up naked on the couch living their best life in a house that does not belong to them. Shondrella takes a shower and came across some clothes to fit her in Magic's room, Clifton did the same in one of the twin's room. Shondrella explained to Clifton what their next move was going to be. They waited for night fall then decide to scroll the neighborhood. The two wore their hats pulled down low trying to disguise themselves much as possible. They walk holding hands like a couple, they were a few steps away from Donald's house. Suddenly BG pulls up full speed directly in front of them, he begins to ask questions. First one was "do you two live around here"? "We are just taking a walk sir, no reason for the integration". Shondrella says. "That's not what I asked". BG stepped out the car and asked for their community badge, the entire community had badges for each household members along with a community key word. BG put that that into place when he became head of the security. BG was a pot head, but he took his job serious. Clifton stated we left our badges at home we will be back to show you". BG said I need you two to stay right here he reached for his phone and for Shondrella arm at the same time. Clifton turned into the hulk he begins to molly wop on BG beating him in the face punch after punch that retarded strength was unreal. Shondrella had to stop him, she grabs his hand and they both take off running back to the Dunlap house. Normally BG would be with his homeboys but tonight he worked alone. BG makes a call to Donald then his boys he explained to them both what just happened. Everybody met up at Donald's Garage. The last thing Courtney wanted to do was call Big C, her sisters and her mom are so extra they take the smallest things and run with it, they will kill over family PERIODT. "I can't believe I let that retard get the jump on me like that BG said". "Man, them retarded mutha fuckas got that never-ending strength, you gone have to knock that nigga out cold; a one hitta quitter". Big C ranted on. "This shit getting out of hand I'm sure that was them two nuts that BG came across so the bitch must be close by, she's some were watching us; I'm going to alert the police". Before Donald could finish Big C said, "hell no bro let's take this bitch down ourselves, we can't keep pussyfooting around with this lunatic". "The police already know what the business is so let's take full advantage make sure they are disabled for life and can't bother this family again". Big C called Caz and gave her the run down then she hit up her two partners in crime, Cotton and Tuesday, Whitney and Camille being their Government. They all were in juvie together and been stuck like glue ever since, laying the smack down on niggas and bitches. Donald turned the gathering into a shindig, he pulled out the grill and started pouring up drinks they were going to pull an all-nighter, no one could sleep they wanted Shondrella, and Clifton caught. Shondrella praised Clifton for his quick thinking. She paced back and forth not knowing what her next move would be she started to panic, so she used Clifton for some sex; normally that helps but this time she seemed worse than usual. She was not giving up she had in her head Donald was going to be hers. "We are going to have to lay low that security guy probably already called the police, so I know it's not safe for us to go back out". Shondrella told Clifton. Clifton asked in his stuttering voice "do do you think the po po police will find us, I don't want to go back". Are we going to sta sta stay in this house"? "I don't know but going back to be chained like an animal is not on my agenda". The two stayed in the house for two days hoping things will blow over, but Donald had beefed up security all blocks were filled with Big C and BG's friends. The police were even riding. Ralph wanted her caught but he did not want her hurt, but he knew shit would get ugly if they caught Shondrella. So, Ralph paid an off-duty cop to circle the neighborhood hourly hoping she would be sighted and brought in. Shondrella knew they could no longer walk the neighborhood, she started looking for keys to one of the cars in the garage. After an hour of searching Clifton spotted some keys in the ignition of a Toyota

Camry, which belongs to Magic's boyfriend Bruce. Bruce car was left there why he joined the Dunlap's on their vacation. Shondrella came across a lock box curiosity got the best of her. Breaking the box open she found two loaded guns, a 25 pistol and a high-power Glock, with boxes of ammo she places the firearms along with the ammo in a book bag she spotted. The power was still off so they had to push the garage door up by hand. They both decide to put on Magic's color wigs one being red the other blue, the two went with different hats trying to downplay their identity. The two pull off and Shondrella being the driver she could not resist going in the direction of Donald's house. Shondrella spots a car pulling out of Donald's driveway she remembers the kind of car Donald drives, so she assumed it was his fiancé, Courtney. After following the car for a few blocks, the confirmation was clear it was indeed Courtney. Courtney exits off the highway and proceed to her destination which was to her wedding planner house to look at some layouts and designs. She first pulls up to a gas station for gas and a Gatorade. While Courtney was in the store purchasing her items, Shondrella pulls up to the pump next to her she tells Clifton exactly what she wanted him to do. Clifton sneaks out the car and begin to hunt his pray. Courtney walks to her car she grabs the nozzle and begin pumping gas. Suddenly out of nowhere Clifton comes from behind he grabs her tight by the mouth with one hand and force her in the car with the other hand. Clifton gets in right beside her. Shondrella speeds off back on the highway, Courtney begins to fight Clifton and screams loud as she could. "HELP, HELP, STOP THIS DAMN CAR"! "Why are you bastards taking me against my will "? After several kicks and punches to Clifton's body he holds her tight with force and tell her to calm down. Shondrella shows her a gun through the review mirror, Courtney begins to beg; "PLEASE LET ME GO, I HAVE A FAMILY PLEASE, I HAVE MONEY I BEG YOU PLEASE". Shondrella speaks up and says" you keep messing around with my man Donald and I do not like that"." Donald is my fiancé we been together since college why do you keep bothering us"? "Donald does not know you nor do he like you, let me help you find a man". "I already have a man and that's Donald". "You need some help he will never be yours you crazy good for nothing bitch, now let me out this damn car". Shondrella then shoots twice through the roof of the car, scaring Courtney and Clifton shitless. "Do not talk to me that way I do not want to hurt you, all I want is my man and you are going to deliver him to me". "You are going to make things worse Donald will never agree to be with you, he's going to call the police and have you locked up"." You can just let me go and we forget about this whole thing, please this is not going to end well". Courtney kept trying to talk her way out of that car while Shondrella drove heading back to the Dunlap house. As they approach the house Courtney says, "why are we at Magic's parents' house"? OMG, this is Bruce car, how the fuck do you know the Dunlap's"? Her questions went unanswered. The garage still was lifted. Shondrella parks the car then Clifton gets out and close the garage door. They all made their way inside the house; Courtney had managed to turn her phone on silent she was waiting for the right time to send a group text to Donald and her sisters. Shondrella told Courtney "do not try anything or I will shoot you with no hesitation". Clifton was looking for some rope in the garage to tie up. Returning with the rope Clifton noticed Shondrella staring at Courtney with much hate, she was thinking in her head what the fuck Donald sees in her. Shondrella had a mean mug plastered on her face and her heart was full of jealousy and hate. After she snapes out of it she checks all the doors and windows why Clifton untangles the rope, Courtney hurries and turns her back away from Clifton, she then sends out a 911 group text that read" I need help that crazy girl Shondella has kidnaped me", "she's with a small frame retarded dude I'm on the next street at the Dunlap's, she has been staying here again". "Hurry she has two loaded guns." Courtney places the phone in her bra under her tits. Shondrella returns and says, "I need you to call my man". Courtney responds by saying "Who is your man"? Shondrella then Slaps hell's fire out of her then screams, "Donald is my man don't you dare play like you don't know that, when he gets here, I'm going to fuck him while you sit there tied up and watch". "With all due respect Donald does not know you so how he is your man"? "Let's be realistic you are infatuated with my fiancé; you're setting yourself up for a major disappointment I PROMISE YOU". "You got your wonder woman cape on with them guns, but you best believe if you put that gun down, I will blaze your ass up" "Just call him so I can talk to him and keep your comments to yourself". "I don't have my phone it was left in my car". "WHAT"? Shondrella screams aloud then give Clifton instructions to go find a phone. "The power is out so, you must use the house phone on the kitchen wall", Courtney said with attitude. Shondrella cuts the rope from Courtney's hands and lead her to the kitchen, Courtney dials the number and the name read twins on Donald's phone he knew it was Courtney. He answers the phone with much attitude Courtney was not able to get out one word, Shondrella snatches the phone out her hand and start telling Donald how much she misses him, and she is in love with him. "I'm not in love with you, you egotistical looney bitch, let Courtney go right now". Donald had made it to the Dunlap's home he runs up to the door beating hard "open the door bitch still on the phone Shondrella says" why are you so mean bae"? I tell you what I'll let this nappy head ass bitch go but only if you agree to leave with me". "O.K. I'll do anything let her go take me I'm the one you want, open the door." Shondrella open the door with gun pointed in Courtney's direction, "strip down so I can make sure you don't have any weapons, Donald did what she said, "ok now go get in your car and Clifton, you follow him". She then walks backwards to the car still pointing the gun at Courtney just then Big C and Cotton and all the sisters pulls up. They all rushed at Shondrella she shot twice in the air after she was secure in the car, she yells for Donald to drive off. Then turned to point the gun directly on him. Courtney called the police and gave them a 10-minute briefing on the situation at hand. No one was hurt from the shots. "Big C begin pacing she mumbled, "I'm gone kill that bitch if that's the last thing I do". "Sis you good that bitch didn't hurt you did she"? "I'm good Chelsea, that is one fucked up chic, she got the game fucked up if she thinks she's going to get my man".

Chapter 11

SHE'S A BIT CRA CRA

THE POLICE HAD ALL the information they needed, there was a statewide search for Shondrella, Clifton and Donald's car. The car was spotted miles away from the Georgia line. Donald had been cursing Shondrella out, "how long do your sick ass think you are going to get away with this, I do not like you I will never like you". He repeated that throughout the ride hoping it would trigger some sense in her brain. "I don't give a fuck how you feel you belong to me, eventually you will grow to love me or that pretty bitch of yours will suffer"." It's a whole team of us, and you best believe I got someone watching that bitch, and they are just as nutty as me waiting for my que to torture her". So, with that being said you will like me, love me and fuck me or a gang of my mentally challenge friends will fuck miss girl, and make her call them daddy". "You better slow your role and watch your fucking mouth when speaking to me". They were about to run out of gas, and no one had any money, all of Donald's belongings were left at the Dunlap's where he was made to strip. Clifton begins to panic acting like a real mental patient, clearly the medication had left his system. Clifton screamed and began scratching on his self he starts to slob; the slob was thick and foamy he was making a noise as if he could not breathe. Shondrella smacks Clifton, she then grabs a water bottle from the cup console and dash some water in his face. She talks soft and delicate while rubbing on his head, he then calms down. Donald had no choice but to make it to the gas station. Donald still was naked meaning he could not get out the car. Shondrella says "I'm about to go in this store and I dare you to move funny my folks are just waiting to ambush your crib on go, so I expect you to behave". Shondrella had some leverage on keeping Donald in line he did not want to chance nothing happening to Courtney he believed Shondrella had more people working with her. Shondrella enters the store she walks up to the counter looking at the young girl's name tag then she says, "Yolanda, I need you to give me your id, the young girl looks at her and says" bitch bye" don't come in here with that drunk shit tonight"! Shondrella repeated it once again this time showing the clerk her gun. The girl reaches for her purse and Shondrella fired a shot "what are you doing bitch? Shonderella screams". The young clerk jumped out of her skin pissing her pants at the same time, she responded with a shaky voice "I'm just getting my ID like you ask I don't want any trouble take what you want and just leave". Yolanda hands over her ID, Shondrella tells her to set the gas pump for a fill up, she then took some drinks and snacks along with the money out the register. When leaving out the door she holds up the ID card and said if you call the cops, it will not be safe at your home. The scared young girl said yes ma'am still shaken up from the shot Shondrella fired. The clerk wanted nothing more than Shondrella to hurry and get out of the store. Shondrella returns to the car and instructs Clifton to pump the gas. While waiting Donald starts talking to Shondrella trying to convince her to let him and his family go he begin to beg, everything Donald was saying sound foreign to her, she was so mesmerized by the motion of his lips and the fact that he was naked that made her moist between her legs.

Chapter 12

DETERMEND

AFTER RIDING FOR ANOTHER hour, they end up at the Quaker Shack a small motel known for drugs and prostitution in Easley S.C. Shondrella used the store clerk ID to get the room she then spots a crack head while walking to the room, she asks him if he had some clothes that she could buy from him. He responded no she showed him a 50-dollar bill, he said "I can go in the big K-Mart and steal you something". "She responded "ok get two men sweat suits that may fit you and one female suit my size; the money will be here when you return". She rushes back to the car to get Donald and Clifton she had them speed walk to the room hoping they was not spotted by anyone especially Donald he still was naked. After 45 minutes in the room Shondrella dozes off leaving Donald and Clifton having a staring match with each other. After hearing a light snore from Shondrella Donald asks Clifton, "how long do you think this shit you doing with her will last"? Clifton says, "I love her she is so nice to me and I don't have anywhere else to go". "I know for a fact this girl is using you if she felt the same way about you, she wouldn't be after me, she needs you, but I need you more I have a family she took me from". "Please let's get out of her together I will vouch for you and say you are totally innocent my brother is a cop he will help you". Donald was saying anything that sounded good. "I don't want to be locked up anymore Shondrella fucks me, and I like it". "That's how she is willing you in, she knows your situation bro, you need your medication you can't go much longer without it before something bad may happen to you". "I promise you I can keep you out of a maximum mental institution and you go to a local group home". Donald continued to whisper encouraging words to Clifton hoping he would be with it. Donald wanted to just rush Shondrella, but she had both guns in her hand, he did not want to risk getting shot. The crackhead whose name was Rick Stone, he was known around Easley as Slick Rick; he was at the big K-Mart about to five finger the clothing items Shondrella requested. He seen a police officer passing out flyers with a picture of Shondrella and a male posted on the flyer the male being Clifton. The flyer said wanted in bold letters and what caught his eye the most was the reward amount 50k. The more he looked around the more cops and helicopters he seen. Slick Rick was no dummy he figured Shondrella was the female that had robbed the USA bank downtown a few days ago. He was about to play her for some money and then turn her in for the reward money. He had the right plan but the wrong female. Slick Rick decided to take this information straight to his boss man and dealer Deuce. Deuce was the man around Easley, he sold mad dope and bitches. Deuce was the biggest money shark and pimp floating these streets, if you looked wrong or out of place you were subject to get fucked up. Deuce had a crew of niggas that eat raw alligator meat and let pit bull dogs bite them for fun. Just bat shit crazy: No body fucked with them they were street bullies and could move mountains in their town. The police did not scare them the police stayed the fuck out of their way if they wanted to make it home to their families. Slick Rick made his way to Deuce main hustle spot on Mayfair Circle he knew it better been some top-notch shit fucking with Deuce at this location. Deuce crew patted Rick down, Slick Rick held up to his name being slick out the mouth, "y'all big buff mutha fuckas patting me down, I'm not packing shit but this long dick". The nigga Moose slapped Rick across his head then took him to Deuce. Rick pulled of the flyer and began to tell him the story at hand, after 15 minutes Deuce sent his right-hand girl Karizma to check things out dismissing Slick Rick as well. Rick followed Karizma to her car as if he were about to get in, she turned around and said, "you better walk your dirty ass to the Shack you will not get in my shit". Karizma arrives at the Shack; she goes in to talk to the clerk Lucy Lou who was down with her crew. "What up Luc"? "what's been cracking around this bitch"? "Same shit different day nothing spectacular helicopters riding looking for some chick who robbed that bank". "I heard the chick is staying here". "What hell naw I would have seen or heard some shit, I just seen on Facebook she robbed another bank in Pickens". "Who is the last female you had check in". "A Yolanda Godfrey". Karizma hands her the flyer is this her"? "Hell, yeah that's her I checked her in like 2 hours ago, she's in room 209". "What the fuck going on Karizma, Lucy asked with a confused face"? Slick Rick walks through the door, Karizma hand motion him over and said, "you were right on everything, I'm about to call Deuce and see how he want us to play this situation". "Remind that nigga of my finder's fee said Slick Rick". "Nigga you know Deuce gone bless you let's keep this on the hush for right now". Karizma instructed them both to keep their eyes on that room and do not let no one in or out, she also sent some more crew members over for extra eyes. Karizma makes a call to Deuce and confirmed that Slick Rick story was indeed all true. "This girl will be more beneficial to us on the street selling pussy and dope verses us turning her in Deuce said". The crew and I are about to come through and get her started on her new career". "Hang tight Karizma I'm headed your way. Shondrella wakes up from her much-needed nap she looks over at Donald; he turns his head rolling his eyes. Shondrella said to the men, "I'm about to go find this nigga with the clothes I'll be right back you two just stay put". Shondrella walks out the door checking her surroundings, after about 60 seconds Donald and Clifton go bolting out the door. Shondrella was still in view of the room she turns around and see them running she pulls out the gun and starts bussing shots; she let off two. Donald kept running but Clifton body fell to the ground both bullets had hit him in the back. Lucy Slick Rick and Karizma came running out the office they bump right into Shondrella. Lucy screams loudly, "what the fuck are you doing bitch"? Shondrella stood there with her mouth open and gun in her hand, Karizma seen shondrella make a move So, she immediately put some air in her chest then football tackled her to the ground and slick rick gained control of the two guns she had. Lucy ran down to Clifton, she yelled out "this man needs some help we got to call an ambulance"." Deuce not going to be happy about this shit," said Lucy. Seconds later Deuce shows up with his entourage of thugs. Karizma filled him in on the action he immediately had his boys grab her up and put her in the ship. The ship was a church van shaped like a ship it was already set up for torture, kidnapping, and all other vicious acts, it was soundproof and untraceable. Deuce did not allow anyone to call the ambulance from the motel instead he had Karizma and Slick Rick drop him off at Easley Emergency Hospital. Karizma did not want Slick Rick in her car but she had no choice, slick Rick got in buckled up and leaned all way back with a Kool-Aid smile. Karizma said "don't get comfortable mutha fucka" she sped off mad she had a dying bloody nigga in the back and a dirty ass bum in the front. No one had notice Donald he had snatched some sheets off a bed while he was running through the motel, he ran to the Speed Mart convenient store screaming to the clerk for a phone he then called Courtney and she was there in less than 30 minutes.

Chapter 13

RUN BOY RUN

COURTNEY PULLS UP TO the address Donald gave her. She was on two wheels driving to the destination, followed by her sisters Big C and Caz and BG, they all were ready for war. On the way back to the house Donald filled Courtney and the rest them in on what went down. Once at the house they called Maxine and Ralph, Donald repeated the story this time he filled them in on Clifton and who he was this whole time. Ralph agreed that if Clifton survived, he would help him stay out of the mental institution. This was important to Donald because he was a man of his word. Maxine was panicking. Even though this was Shondrella's mess that was still her daughter and watching and listening to people drag her name her attitude was on 1000. She was even more mad with Ralph feeling like he was siding with strangers. Maxine ended up snapping on Big C, who in return slapped her so hard she flopped backwards. The shit looked like what Ike did to Tina's girl Jackie in the restaurant of What's love got to do with it. Before it could go any further Ali grabbed Maxine calming her down while the sisters and their mom grabbed Big C. "Some shit I just don't play about and my sister is one of them, I don't give a fuck who that retarded bitch belong to; she got a one-way ticket to hell fucking with me", Big C threatened. The police were called and informed on the situation they were so familiar with; shit was about to get real they knew they had to apply pressure and catch Shondrella at this point. Clifton was in ICU unconscious after having emergency surgery to remove the bullets from his back. As of now Shondrella was being blamed for multiple counts of attempted murder, aggravated assault, resisting arrest, and a few other charges. She was considered armed and dangerous. Regardless of Ralph's connections the police were ordered to proceed with caution and was given the greenlight to use force if need be. Ralph called his street connections to hit the streets to find out how he could have a sit down with Deuce. He had to get Shondrella before the law did. Even though she brought this on herself he could not let her die, he was strong on family he wanted her locked up but not dead. Monica had given him an ultimatum with his involvement with Shondrella and Maxine, the shit had gotten out of hand. Monica and Ralph could not enjoy their life because the two of them were always getting into something, and Ralph being the big brother he always put his cape on and rescue them.

-Deuce attempts to turn Shondrella out but his torture methods do not work, Shondrella is cut from a different cloth, she is crazy to the highest power she is no stranger to pain and lives for the exact shit Deuce was dishing out. When he attempts to rape her and send multiple men in to do the same, she ends up blowing his mind and the men as well. Fucking them like a porn star doing tricks and flexing muscles she did not know she had, her pussy became a suctional vacuum. Them niggas had never been fucked like that before. She made sure to put that extra arch in her back and throw her pussy extra hard when she was with Deuce. Shondrella had been a sex nympho since a young girl, she was not allowed to have any animals due to her high sexual fantasies. She would fuck their dog and cat, and often played in her pussy while watching Pinky get fucked on porn hub. The more the men beat and fuck her the more she liked it, she did not flinch from the abuse. It was actually a turn on for Deuce, after she sucked the skin off his dick, he was sold. Shondrella had a high tolerance for sex and pain, Deuce was fighting a losing battle trying to damage her. Deuce begins to like Shondrella and develop a deep infatuation for her, Shondrella's pussy felt like warm melted butter to Deuce he had never had no pussy as good as hers. She convinces Deuce to help her get to Donald promising him Courtney and all the sisters in exchange. Shondrella had Deuce look the girls up on Facebook and he was all in. Shondrella and Deuce begin to work side by side he even used her for a few of his heavy hits when he normally would only use his bottom bitch Karizma. Karizma is not to happy about Shondrella, because she was his right hand and had worked hard for that spot, only to be kicked to the curb. Deuce had moved all the business to a far-off motel because the police were looking for Shondrella and the bank robber around the clock. It was to much heat to continue with business at the Quake Shack. Karizma did something she never thought she would do she reached out to Slick Rick. "What the fuck this bitch got on Deuce Rick"? "I don't know but he let me fuck her and that pussy is FYE and the head even better she got that snap". "But I do smell trouble". "Come ride with me so I can go dig around at the hospital and find some information out on this mystery bitch", "oh shit I get an invite to ride in the whip Slick Rick said excitedly". "Nigga bring your dirty ass on we making a stop at the trap so you can take a fucking bath and change clothes, you been wearing them clothes for two damn years through the summer, winter, and fall". Slick Rick got into the car feeling sad. Karizma knew she would need Slick Rick, so she took a detour after Rick was done bathing, she gave him lotion something he probably had not used since grade school. Karizma also gave Rick a polo sweat suit and a pair of timberland boots, he had fresh sock and boxers. Rick had on a pair of tightie whities that was so black and soiled they look like motor oil was cleaned up with them. She arranged for him a haircut and face shape up. On the way to the hospital, she reaches in her glove compartment and hand him a pinky diamond ring and adjustable mouth gold top grill. Slick Rick was made over, looking like a million bucks. "Look nigga Karizma said seriously this ring and grill is yours to keep if you pawn or sell it, I will cut you off forever". "This is the beginning of a new life for you". Karizma gave Rick a motivational speech all the way to the hospital, she had amped Rick up to change his life around. Slick Rick cried softly looking in the car mirror amazed on how good he looked, he could not remember the last time he had a bath and brushed his teeth. He stepped out the car like a boss feeling so fresh and so clean no grit between his ass, he no longer had that itchy walk. He was looking sharp as a thumb tack. On the elevator going to the ICU floor Rick grabs Karizma giving her a bear hug saying thank you over and over. The ICU floor was packed with reporter's case managers from the mental institution along with the police and FBI. Clifton was given a blood transfusion; the breathing tubes will be taken out if he rests well through the night. The surgeon announced with a few months of rehab he should be good as new the bullets missed his spine by a centimeter. It did not take long for Karizma and Rick to find out what they needed to know about Shondrella, they gathered lots of tea and could not believe the shit they were hearing; they both spoke with Donald and several others. Now they know the severity of the situation, they are dealing with a certified live wire.

Chapter 14

CAPTAIN SAVE A HOE

AFTER RECEIVING INFORMATION ON how Shondrella was turning tricks and hustling for Deuce. Ralph demanded his connects to make this meeting happen ASAP. He had to do what he could to save his niece. He wanted her medicated and in a hospital. Not dead, in jail, or turning tricks on the street. He knew that it was only a matter of time before her delusions got her into even more trouble than she was already in. Deuce and Ralph linked up at a Starbucks right off the Dacusville highway in Easley. Ralph was older than Deuce, but he was no slow cookie when it came to the streets. Ralph went in headfirst. "Look Deuce I'm not going to sit here and sugar coat shit, I have done my homework on you and being the man that you are I know you have done the same". "I respect you and your hustle and will never try to interfere on how you eat". However, I do have receipts that you have my niece Shondrella;" I do not know what she has done to you for you to have a hold on her and using her for your business". "My niece is terribly ill she also is the most wanted fugitive in America right now. Shondrella is only going to draw attention and slow your operation down maybe even shut it down if you don't let her go". "I would like to say it's a pleasure even being in your presence, a top-notch attorney mixed with some street causalities". "your credentials speak for its self-Mr. Ralph". I on the other end do not want any beef, I have a multimillion-dollar operation to run and quarterback". "Shondrella is fine she is not hurt and I'm not holding her against her will". "I can assure you she will not be harmed but I'm not letting her go". "I would like for you to get me her medication so she can stay on track. I deeply feel she would be better off with me making money than locked up in some mental institution like a fuckan lab rat". "You shouldn't want her in jail either Mr. Ralph, so just be easy while she rocks out here with me". "She fucked up more times than usual; and may need special attention but that's not a reason to give her to the state". "You really need to think this through Ralph said with a shaky voice, I guarantee you she's plotting on you right now". "This is for best I know you are too deep in the game to put 12 on me, so just trust me your niece is better off with me, I will take good care of her". "So, get me a year supply of all her medication and just know she is safe, I will contact you if I need you". Ralph was not about to go into a back-and-forth battle with Deuce, so he decided to just walk off, he mumbled to himself "this mutha fucka don't know what he in for". Donald was happy to be home, but he was saddened by Clifton being shot, He was not so mad at Clifton because he knew he was coached and forced by the grimiest mental patient ever. Courtney and her sisters were plotting to get Shondrella, Big C had people looking for her all over Easley, the sisters had the taste of blood in their mouth for Shondrella. Courtney was about to become a mental patient herself she felt as if this girl was controlling her love life by her obsession over Donald. "Donald is my man why the fuck this crazy bitch want leave us alone, I want this bitch caught, dead I don't give a fuck I won't to watch this nut bucket ass bitch burn". Courtney cried out to her sisters; they all are feeling her pain with thoughts of killing Shondrella on their mind. Shondrella had gained a small fan base from the niggas and bitches she been sexing up, not to mention she had Deuce in her side pocket too. She had people watching Donald and Courtney's every move, she now had plans to target Courtney. Shondrella had been engaging in sexual roll play and group sex with one of the head Doctor's at Easley Emergency Center, Dr. Racqi Sparks. He was married to Debbie Sparks she was a Doctor as well; she was also getting some of Shondrella cookies and love action. Shondrella had sessions with them both on the same days and they never crossed paths or found out about the other. Shondrella had one of her sex clients Samp to follow Courtney on her way to work, the purpose was for him to cause a car wreck to run his truck into her car with enough force to make her need medical attention. The truck Samp was driving had a big metal frame kit across the front-end that could put a deer flat on its back. Samp goes around Courtney on the highway to move ahead of her. He then waits on her to bypass him while she was driving forward, he pulls out from the right side and smashes into the passenger side causing her to slide across the highway being hit by two other cars. Samp then moves his way out of traffic speeding to his destination. Fire trucks, Ambulance and Police all arrive on the scene, Courtney was rushed to Easley Emergency. Samp had sent Dr. Racqi a thumbs up text alerting him that the job was done, and Courtney would be arriving soon by Ambulance. Dr. Racqi will be the leading attending physician to handle Courtney's injuries. The police had contact Donald and Sabrina giving them the graphics of the accident. On the way to the hospital Sabrina calls the sisters and Donald calls his mom and brother Alvin. Once they all arrived everyone was in a panic, Donald rushes to the desk with Sabrina on his heels. He asks the nurse "can you please get me some information on my fiancé Courtney Mims"? "I received a call from the police she was in a car accident". The nurse was nice and responded, "yes sir we have several traumas at the moment let me find out what I can for you". Sabrina fell to her knees praying out loud "(LORD PLEASE WATCH OVER MY BABY LET HER BE OK, GIVE ME STRENGTH LORD OH MY BABY".) She cried her eyes out, all the sisters were holding her and comforting each other at the same time. Just when their patients were wearing thin from not hearing back from the nurse Dr. Racqi walks up. "Mims family; yes, is my fiancé ok Doctor Donald yells out so close to his face he could kiss him. "Your fiancé has been banged up pretty bad she is in surgery right now from the chart update I could see her shoulder has been shifted out of place and she has a broken arm, from the looks of things nothing seems to be too critical ". "But lets just wait until we have all the labs, and she is out of surgery before we claim victory". "I am sorry to inform you there can only be one family member here on this floor, the rest of the family must wait in the designated area downstairs; I am Dr. Racqi feel free to have me paged if you need anything or have any further questions". Sabrina insisted on Donald staying, the rest of the gang went downstairs to make phone calls. Hours later the entire downstairs waiting area is flooded with family and friends praying and fellowshipping Courtney comes out alright. After Courtney lab results were in Dr. Racqi discover that she is pregnant, so he was not about to do what Shondrella wanted him to do and that was to poison her blood with a serum that will cause her to become mute and paralyze. Shondrella was not happy about the feedback Dr, Racqi gave her, he had some dignity and he refused to harm an unborn child. Dr. Racqi moves slowly to the waiting room where Donald was sitting in the chair with his leg shaking like a stripper, when he noticed Dr. Racqi coming his way he stood up. "Your fiancé will recover simply fine; she does have a broken arm and a torn rotator cuff she has several bruises from the glass and air bags. She is in tremendous pian, we can only give her lower doses of pain medication because she is pregnant". Donald says out loud "pregnant are your serious". "Yes, sir Congratulations, we need to keep her in recovery for 4 hours then she will be transported to a regular room". "Thank you so much Doc tell the whole surgery team thanks for all they did to save my fiancé, my family and I are greatly appreciated to you all", Donald said while holding back tears he was filled with an overdose of excitement.

$$Chapter\ 15$$

WHEN THE MYSTERY UNFOLDS

TWO WEEKS HAS PAST, and they now know that the wreck was no accident. The police gave the family the details they had from other drivers that was on the same highway Courtney was driving. A red flag immediately popped up with the family, this had Shondrella written all on it. Courtney was now home starting her recovering process. She begged her boss and Donald to let her go back to work, she hated feeling helpless, so she spent hours rehabbing her arm and shoulder trying to rush the recovery. Donald was stuck on NO! Hell NO! but they compromised with her doing minimal work from home. She reasoned that it would help her stay sane. She was dealing with a lot mentally and physically; she had begun to think she was a damn mental patient. What should be her happiest moments in life was her worst nightmare. She was in terrible pain, pregnant, engaged and being hunted by the craziest bitch on this earth. Courtney sat and cried her eyes out just thinking about what she did to deserve this shit. She did not bother anyone and always tried to help people. A part of her understood Shondrella was mentally off balanced however, the other part of her did not give a flying fuck. Courtney felt like Shondrella had to be stopped permanently. Her sisters were there to wait on her hand and foot per Donald's orders. What Donald did not know was that her sisters were helping her plot on a way to turn this around on Shondrella to make her pay. Big C reached out to Karizma, who she knew from juvie. Karizma agreed to meet with Big C and Courtney. Since the block was hot, they met up at a truck stop at the Georgia, South Carolina border. "Hey girl, hey", Big C said giving Karizma a hug. They were cool but still on guard considering they were technically on different sides. Courtney sat and listened as the two women started talking like they were best friends. They were speaking in code, and Courtney picked up on it right away. She just sipped her coffee and ate her pie while listening intently. After ending the meeting everyone went their separate ways, literally in different directions in case they were being followed. Big C drove the next hour or so to Commerce GA for a little retail therapy. On the way she explained to Courtney that she and Karizma were bunk mates with a girl named Tracy Fleming, who went by Trix. Trix was the bank robber. The plan was to reach out to her with an escape plan. If she agreed they were going to set Shondrella ass up to take the fall for the bank robbery while helping Trix escape to Mexico. Sabrina and the rest of the sisters met them at the outlets where they all tried to cheer Courtney up. They spent racks of cash and just bullshitted around like they used to do. On the ride back, Big C filled the other sisters in on what she called operation "Get rid of Shondrella's crazy ass." Courtney's medication had worn off and she was in pain, they had over did it for today, so they rushed to get her home before Donald flipped out and put an APB out on them.

Meanwhile, back in Greenville, Donald is with his brother Alvin. Donald needed a break for himself. He was trying to be strong for Courtney and handle this shit like a man, but it was weighing him down. He got a call from the hospital regarding Courtney's lab results, so he and his brother went to pick them up. "I got a weird ass feeling something not right bro, I feel some bullshit in the mix. I am so sick of this shit with this dum dum ass bitch. I lowkey wanna just pick up and move but this bitch crazy enough to follow us and then what? I won't have any back up." Donald vented to his brother as he rode passenger. Alvin just listened to his baby brother, while he was formulating a plan himself. He came off as emotionless, but he adored his brother. He would do anything to make sure he could continue his strait-laced life. Alvin felt like it was his duty as a big brother. "It's gonna be alright bro. You gotta keep your head up. We Cannot fight crazy with crazy. Not this kinda crazy anyway", Alvin stated while pulling up to Easley Emergency. The brothers walked in and asked the receptionist for Dr. Debbie Sparks. "Fourth floor, and to the right", she stated while eyeing Alvin. He winked in response and they walked in silence. Alvin said to Donald "bro this here is crazy because why would they not call Courtney for her results and call you, you two are not married yet and lab results are confidential last I known". Donald responded, "you are so right bro they can't just exclude Courtney and come straight to me". Donald was nervous, his gut was telling him that something was about to go down. "Good afternoon doctor", Donald greeted as he walked in and sat down. "Afternoon gentlemen and call me Debbie, please". "So, what's up doc?" Alvin stated getting straight to business. Debbie looked at Donald then at Alvin before speaking. "Umm, Donald what I have to tell you is confidential, you may want to receive this in private." "Well, if it's so damn confidential why the hell Courtney not here receiving her own results, Alvin said with a mug on his face". Donald's heart sank, he could not take any more bad news. "This is my brother and Courtney his family too, just come on with the come on no need to stall". "Alright then sir, let me grab my paperwork", Debbie handed Donald a paper, "What you have in your hands are all the labs that were tested for Ms. after her accident. Alvin remained quiet but he was scoping everything and everyone in the room. He was good at reading people, and he did not like what he was picking up on in the room. He decided it was best to wait to act on his feelings. Debbie continued; "It is standard practice to test young women that come in with Courtney's demographics for pregnancy, and all STDs and STIs. As you know she is pregnant. We have found that she has a bad UTI as well as a positive gonorrhea and chlamydia test". Donald stood up quickly balling up the paper and walked out of the office. Alvin was soon to follow, but not before he picked up on the smirk on Debbie's face. Dr. Racqi had no play in this, Shondrella wanted him to poison Courtney's blood and have her paralyzed. Once her labs showed her being pregnant, he backed out he was not about to harm an unborn child. So Shondrella and his wife planned to tell Donald this bogus story, Shondrella felt like it would break them up and give her this happy ending with Donald. Debbie laughed as Donald left the room in a rage.

When they got to the car, Alvin let Donald have a few minutes to himself. He had not seen his brother cry since they were kids and he refused to see it today. "Aye imma go make a call. Be right back". Donald cried. He was so hurt; how could she do this to him. He had so many questions, and to top it all off this crazy bitch was stalking him.

He was about to call Courtney, but his brother walked back up and got in the car. "Before you do or say anything. THINK!", Alvin stressed to him. "Don't be reactive bro. Especially not right now, with everything going on." Donald nodded with a sigh, and texted Courtney instead.

WE GOTTA TALK

After that he put his phone on Do Not Disturb and rode the rest of the ride in silence. He could not go home and face Courtney at the moment, so he went to Alvin's crib to chill which was right around the corner.

Maxine is mad at the world right now. She is barely talking to her brother and has stopped talking to Courtney or Donald. Partly because she was embarrassed and the other part because she actually wanted to help Shondrella. She was her only daughter after all. Maxine's problem was, she felt like Shondrella's mental state was all her fault, so she had a guilty mind that led her to keep helping Shondrella, thinking she was supporting her. As fucked up as that sounds, that was her justification. She went driving through Easley looking for Deuce, and not being smart about it either. Soon as she gave up, she stopped for food at the Hamburger hut When she got back in her car she was not alone. Deuce was not the kind of person you just ask for and not get an answer. Two of his goons forced Maxine to drive to a secret location to meet with the boss. Maxine was scared to death, but she had to put her big girl panties on and face this man. She needed her daughter she was not willing to lose her baby girl. While Maxine stated her case and begged for him to release her child, Deuce fantasized about turning Maxine out. He figured Shondrella's freak had to come from somewhere, who better than the mama. He knew he could get a good bit of money for a mother daughter duo. Only thing stopping him was Ralph. He did not need that nigga sniffing around his operation for his sister and his niece. That was trouble he did not want or need so he left his thoughts in his head. "Ms. Maxine, like I told your brother, Shondrella Is not being held against her will"." I will not allow her to leave at this moment". "No harm will come to her, but she is better off with me". I do not want to see her locked away". "However, I understand the situation, so I will allow you to see her." Maxine's face lit up. "Thank you so much", she cried. She went quietly and willingly with the goons as they blindfolded her and escorted her to another location. When the blindfolds came off, she was sitting in front of Shondrella. She looked different. Crazier than she had ever seen, and totally off medication. It appeared that she had had a total mental break. Maxine begs Shondrella to just run away with her. She is worried that Shondrella will be hurt because so many people were looking for her. Shondrella runs a quick guilt trip on her mom telling her that she feels abandoned and neglected. She plays on Maxine's feelings and get her to feel bad so she can manipulate her. Maxine cannot see what she is doing. Shondrella had Maxine snitching on everyone. By the time Maxine was done talking and ready to leave she had sold everyone out, from Ralph having people looking for her, to Big C plotting something. Although she did not know as much as Shondrella would have liked; she was still giving out useful information.

Ralph had a client of his who worked in pharmaceuticals get a decent supply of medications together for Shondrella. Even though he had people following her and Deuce around, a part of him hoped that she was better off with Deuce and that he could finally wash his hands of the situation. He sat at his desk in deep thought. He knew it was going to get worse before it got better. His only concern now was his sister. He knew how Maxine was about Shondrella. Hell, the apple did not fall far from the tree, and Maxine was lowkey looney too. She just not medication looney. He answered his phone with a simple "Yeah" and he listened. One of his street soldiers was calling to tell him they saw Maxine with Deuce and Shondrella.

Karizma gets Slick Rick a job. He will be working as a janitor at the hospital. It is a legit job, but it is a favor. In return he must report back to her and her only, all things he can muster up about Shondrella. He will be able have eyes on Clifton as well while working. His job is to gather information and make sure Clifton is on their side in putting a stop to Shondrella. One day while Slick Rick was working, he overheard Racqi and Debbie in and all-out battle about what Shondrella wanted them to do next. Shondrella exposed the couple with each other's secret she felt they would work better together on what she wanted. Dr. Racqi however had a change of heart. He had Deuce give him another trick, he cut Shondrella off all together. Slick Rick did not think the conversation was important until Racqi said, "Deb I really don't give a fuck what her head game is like, I refuse to help her ruin anymore lives." Common sense told Rick they were discussing Shondrella. Slick Rick then reports to Karizma. Karizma phones Big C who was over at Alvin's crib they were trying to shine some light on this this whole STD shit. Karizma told Big C she was on her way with some tea. Big C was in a rage "I don't know what the fuck is going on Donald, but my sister does not have no fucking STD this shit is bogus". She has never been with any other man but you, you took her fucking virginity nigga so it's either you gave it to her or somebody lying". They all sit in Alvin kitchen around the island passing a blunt around quiet as a mouse. Suddenly the doorbell ring it was Karizma and Slick Rick. Alvin opens the door greeting them by saying "wud up fam". Karizma and Slick Rick gave a head nod then b-lined to the kitchen with the others. "Pass me that blunt bitch this shit here is some hot tea". "How about the crazy bitch is fucking the Doctors at Easley Emergency. Racqi and Debbie Sparks, they are husband and wife they both been buying tricks from Deuce for years". I know them personally they have done mad favors in the past for us". Karizma went on in critique details, now the pieces of the puzzle were connecting. "I told you bro that shit was fake as fuck; by law, no doctor can expose a patients lab work, that bitch thinks she has all the sense in the world" Alvin said while moving around the kitchen showing emotion. "We need to get this bitch she doing the most" we cannot let Courtney find out she's already on edge" said Donald. "How The fuck are we going to make it pass Deuce" Big C added. "Leave Deuce to Slick Rick and I, you guys may not be punks, but Deuce is in the major leagues". "He has so many people on his pay roll You would have to have an inside connection in order to get arm's length of him; Karizma went over her plan with a grimy smirk on her face. Karizama knew exactly what she had to do to get her spot back, she really did not care as much about being around Deuce she misses that power and control. She had been Deuce's bottom bitch since jellies and bobo's, she was the one running shit you had to go through her to get to Deuce. Now Shondrella was in the driver seat and she did not like it one bit.

Chapter 16

CHOP CHOP

KARIZMA AND SLICK RICK had stopped by to catch up with
Deuce. Deuce had not seen Slick Rick since his makeover. "Damn my
nigga you look nice cleaned up, I see you haven't been at the trap buying
and begging". Deuce had to add that part in, "Hell naw nigga this the
new me it feels good to be drug free, if I can stop smoking these damn
Newport's I'll be doing championship good"." Nigga while you got
jokes, I got a pocket full money an honest paying job shot out to your
girl for believing in me". "Well damn, I would have never imagined this
one", said Deuce. "I remember her cursing me out for you having me
ride on jugs with her, now what's this all of a sudden you two are besties,
Collaborating and playing patty cake and shit". "I always knew Rick
could do well he just needed that push can't smoke crack forever nigga".
"Well, I'm gone need you to stop being captain save a hoe before I end
up broke". They all shared a long laugh. Karizma asked Deuce what
needed to be done before she handles the first of the month count and
reup. He gave her a sad look then said "Shondrella has already taken
care of that love but here is your cut". "I been doing the reups since Black
Rob said whoa nigga, now you got this looney toon doing my job; really
Deuce". Karizma got up and walked out Slick Rick was right behind
her until Deuce called him back, he had a job for Rick. When Rick
heard what it was, he was all smiles. Rick was assigned to drive the girls
to their designated spot for tricks, and make sure they stay safe. Blossom
one of the tricks was up first she had a call at the Covington Hotel in
Mauldin. While she went to handle her business, Rick sends one of his
men he had tag alone to go stand outside the door for her safety. He

then tells the other two girls to go take a walk, so he could be alone with Shondrella. "All you had to do was say you wanted some pussy nigga", Shondrella said to Rick while she unbuckles his pants and pulls out his dick. "Actually, I just wanted to talk but since you got it out let me see what that mouth do". Shondrella gives Rick some nasty wet sloppy toppy she then places a condom on his dick and took him for the ride of his life, Rick was done in from the head because he nutted in 3 minutes flat. "Damn nigga I'm glad I got a call to go to that was a waste of ass, are you done". "Girl you know your pussy good I couldn't hold it, let me rejuvenate then ill fuck your back out". "you know I'm working with a monster". Shondrella laughed while she wiped herself clean with some baby wipes. "So, what you wanted to talk about" Shonderrella asked sarcastically with and inquiring mind". "Nothing major just wanted to chop it up with you". "Well let's see if your conversation can last longer than them strokes". "Stop with the jokes, you're going to hurt my male ego". "But anyway, I see you handling things around the way what kind of plans you got"? "What you mean"? "Are you planning on being with Deuce or you just going to sell pussy forever". "No Deuce is going to help me get the love of my life Donald, I just got to help him first". "I hope you don't believe that shit you have sold your soul to the devil you belong to Deuce now; he's making paper off of you there is no way he will let you go". "The only way out is to escape". "How will I do that with all of his men around, I'm always being watched". "Thursday is meeting day none of the men will be at the house. Deuce will be alone, use what he like most and catch him of guard, your pussy is powerful fuck that nigga until he passes out then kick rocks". "Deuce has threatened me, and I have seen what he does to the enemy, for once in my life I am scared". "Well do what a scared woman would do and get the fuck out of there this will be your only chance". Slick Rick continued to talk to Shondrella in between stops he felt he had got in her head he sent Karizma a text telling her she went for it, that was Karizma plan to get Rick to get inside her head. It was now Tuesday two days before Shondrella had to decide if she was going to bounce or not. Shondrella walks in the room and she see Deuce getting some head from Blossom he was enjoying it to the fullest. She did not know how to take that because since she came around Deuce had only been fucking her, she was the only one being allowed to suck his dick. She was getting Royal treatment in her book and for her to get script from that she felt some type of way. Shondrella storms out the room and go to her room where she paced back and forth. She begins to scratch her arm aggressively until blood starts to pour out, she made loud noises that caught Deuce attention a few times. She pulls her hair out in patches; she is banging her head against wall speaking what seems to be a foreign language. As the day moves forward Shondrella continues with weird outburst. Deuce starts to keep a close eye on her; he starts to rethink about having her around he is low key scared she may have a psychotic mental break down. Deuce has seen firsthand her displaying some violent and strange behavior, he starts to think back of the conversations Ralph and Maxine warned him about. Wednesday comes and Shondrella notice that Blossom was taking her spot. Blossom had been doing all the transactions and making moves she normally would do. Shondrella was now more than convinced on what she had to do. She locked herself in her room until thursday. Today was the day, Shondrella was up early dressed sexy as ever. She sat in a chair in her room and rock back and forth in complete silence. Soon as the men left, she made her way to Deuce room. He looks her over and she licks her lips, and he was immediately sold she toys around with him until she had him naked. "I was becoming a bit worried about you, but I see what it is now", you miss this dick in your mouth". "Don't you ever worry Blossom will never handle this dick like you". She sucks his dick nice and slow until she gets him completely relaxed, his dick is now at full attention, Deuce yells out "fuck girl you miss this dick huh, that mouth so wet I'm about to skeet all down your throat". Shondrella feels around in her bra with one hand moments later she pulls out a box cutter. Shondrella holds his dick in the choke hold position, while her mouth is still gripped around the head of his dick. She then quickly cut his dick completely off, Shondrella dropped the box cutter and tuned away and did not look back. She grabs a duffle bag full of money out of Deuces closet then she takes off out the door. Little did she know Big C, Donald, Alvin, Karizma and Slick Rick were waiting on side of the house for her. Soon as she ran out the house Big C smashed her across the face with a cement block a perfect TKO. They drag her to the car and tie up her hands and feet. Karizma heard screaming from Deuce in the house, she runs in the house and followed the sounds of the screams. She finds him flat on his back looking half dead holding his hand across what use to be his dick. Deuce screams were at a high pitch, his voice would crackle when he starts to fade in and out of consciousness. Karizma mouth is open wide, she is in shock and grossed out by the scenery. "OMG nigga this bitch just Lorena Bobbitt your ass". Karizma manages to phone the others telling them what Shondrella had done to Deuce. Donald grabs his dick and make a slight frown. "put the nigga dick in a plastic bag on ice and take him to the ER". "We are going to continue with our plan". "Y'all eighty-six that bitch" Karizma responded. Caz and Z.Z. two of Courtney's sisters were in a secret location waiting on the others to arrive they had dug up a grave and was going to bury her alive. 45 minutes later they pull up to the location Shondrella starts to wake up Big C points a gun directly in her face "You just couldn't leave my sister alone could you, I want to blow your mutha fuckan brains out but that's too easy for you". Shondrella spits in Big C face Big C beats her unconscious with her pistol, Alvin had to intervene and stop her. Shondrella was pulled out the car. Caz begin to pour honey all over her body while Z.Z. grabs a crab crate. They place her body in the crate while dumping fire ants and baby mice on top of her, you would think you were watching an episode of Fear Factor. The top piece to the crate had a round stick light bulb and a picture of Courtney glued to the inside top crate. The plan was to torture her even more, looking at Courtney's picture while her life is about to expire. This was definitely a double whammy. They nail the crate closed and place her in the made grave. They waited until she became conscious again, then the men proceed to shovel the dirt on top of her until the job was complete. Shondrella squirms around and screams loudly, the crew ignored her and once the job was done, they all drove off. They were all in agreeance that burring her was the only way to eliminate the problem she was worse than a boomerang she kept coming back, if there was a mental obsession award, she would win hands down. They all vowed to never speak on what just happed ever again. Ralph men still were undercover following Shondrella's ever move, waiting for the right time to snatch her up but they were unsuccessful. The men had a visual on where they had taken Shondrella but just could not make out what was going on without blowing their cover. Once the coast was clear the two men went to the spot where Shondrella was buried. They were not sure what they were looking at. They knew they were in the right spot but, had no clues or signs of Shondrella. Unsure of what happened; the men kept looking high and low searching all surrounding areas. After coming up with nothing the men agreed to call Ralph. "Yeah boss, I think them sisters did something to Shondrella.", one of the men said into the phone. Ralph asked him to explain what all had taken place. He kept his cool on the phone, but he was panicking on the inside. Although their action was justified, he still did not like the shit, he was all tapped out on getting involved with her and Maxine's nonsense. The heat between he and his wife Monica was becoming outrageous and aggravating, the tension was so thick you could cut it with a knife. He told his men to continue to search the area and wait for him to show back up.

Ralph goes to check on Courtney. He was genuinely concerned about her wellbeing and he needed to know if she was the reason for her sisters' attack on his niece. While he was talking to her Donald and the others showed up. Everyone acted as if nothing was wrong. He could pick up on the tension between Donald and Courtney. After making some small talk Ralph asked to talk to Donald in private. "Sure, thing let me use the bathroom first", Donald replied as he walked off. Ralph asked Courtney "what's all the tension about with her and Donald"? She shrugged her shoulders and began to cry. "He had the audacity to question my loyalty to him". Apparently, some fuck face ass doctor called to meet with him, giving him paperwork and lab results saying I have a STD'. "They found out the doctor was bogus, but he should have been on my side regardless of what a mutha fucka say". Ralph nodded his head in understanding, putting pieces together in his head. "I have never been with anyone but Donald". "He was my first ever, Courtney cries got a little louder. "Donald heard her in the bathroom he dropped his head. "I know Shondrella has something to do with this, but I can't prove it". Ralph stood up and told Courtney to take it easy, and that things would get better soon. Donald and Ralph walked outside to speak in private. "Look man, Imma keep it a buck with you". I don't know exactly what you did with my niece but that's blood, so I need you to let me know her whereabouts and what you guys did NOW." Ralph cut straight to the chase. Donald was caught off guard but did not say a word. He just stared off into space not really knowing what to do anymore. This was taking a toll on him. Ralph looked at him in pity and offered him some manly advice. "Nigga you know like everyone else knows that your girl is only your girl". "She ain't never been with another nigga so act like it". Yeah, you got the results from a crooked doctor and that shit scared you, but you got to tighten the fuck up." Donald gave Ralph a crazy frowned look. "Yeah, I know almost everything, I make it my business", he laughed. "You think you are hurt because you thought she cheated; she is crushed because you didn't believe in her enough to know that shit was a lie. Your girl is making herself sick, carrying your baby and dealing with my fucked-up family". "End this go put your best apology game on; comfort her and most of all tell her you will never doubt her again". "If Joe Biden himself is against her you better be with her". "Do not let Shondrella make you someone you're not, tell me what y'all did to my niece". "Look man everything you just said was true indeed". "I appreciate the motivational speech, but I don't know shit about your niece". "What I do know is; I hope the bitch never comes back and leave my fiancé and I the fuck alone". "I don't think you want to play this game with me young man, all I ask is for you to tell me what y'all did". "If she dead she dead she brought that on herself, but I need to know". "With all due respect I would like for you to leave my home please and do not return". Ralph respectfully walked away but that would not be the last time Donald, or his family see him. Ralph did not fault anyone for handling their business, he knew she was a hand full, he just wanted closure and he felt like he had to get it. Shondrella was recking havoc on everyone, Ralph was going to get old a gray before time if he does not leave his family alone.

Chapter 17

SHE JUST WON'T STOP

MAXINE WAS SITTING ON the patio smoking a blunt and drinking a bottle of Moscato when Ralph got to his house. "Wassup sis? What you got going on", he tried to sound as nonchalant as possible, but he could see the change in his sister, and he was scared. He felt her slipping mentally and there was nothing he could do about it. He knew in his heart that if something bad happened to Shondrella, Maxine would more than likely lose herself totally "Them bitches did something to my baby bro, I know it", she calmly said while exhaling and passing the gas. "How you figure?", playing dumb, he accepted the blunt and sat down. He listened to his sister for the next 30 minutes. During that time, he learned that Maxine had been in touch with Shondrella and that they were planning to run. He was able to put the entire story together and was disappointed in himself and his bloodline for how things went sideways. "Sis, you can't beat yourself up about this. You did the best you could given the situation". "No one can ever fault you for that.". That was all he had to say on the situation. Once they finished smoking Ralph went to take a shower, he needed to process all of this. When he woke up this morning, he had no idea the day would be that eventful. Stepping out of the shower he saw a notification come through his phone. It was his men letting him know there was some development on the situation. "Here we go", he said to himself as he dialed the number. "Talk to me, and make it quick", he instructed. "Boss, we got a problem". "We didn't find anything earlier, but we kept looking". "We ended up having to go back to the car because a white family was bird watching and we looked suspicious". "Their dog started barking, going fuckan hay wire". "Long story short, we at the hospital". "Shondrella is in ICU". "The white people found her." Before he could even process what was going on Maxine spoke. "What happened to my baby"? What the fuck going on"? "Did somebody do something to my baby?" She got hysterical quick "Which hospital"? "Send me the other information". "I'm on the way", Ralph barked speaking in code about the information form the white family. He knew he would have to keep a close eye on this. He did not need any of this coming back to him. "I'm driving", he looked at Maxine and spoke. "Do me a favor, please, do not nut up in these people hospital". "Let me see what I can find out first". "You gotta be smart about this one sis ok", he asked his sister. She was in the passenger seat hugging herself and mumbling "No No No not my baby" repeatedly. Ralph made sure to keep all if his information to himself, he knew he would have hell keeping Maxine off Courtney and her sisters if she found out they had something to do with this. He himself was upset but he knew she earned everything anyone did to her because she did much worse.

When they arrived at the hospital it was total chaos. Apparently, everyone needed an ER that day, the waiting room was packed. Ralph was able to sweet talk the charge nurse, so they were not waiting long before they got the status on Shondrella. She was ICU, unresponsive, on a ventilator. She had coded once already. Her body had gone into shock and sepsis started to set in. She was allergic to the honey and the bites from the mice and fire ants did nothing but speed the anaphylaxis up. She was in a medically induced coma to ease the pain while the doctors did all they could for her. Maxine broke down crying while Ralph held her. He had called Ali to come through for her but had no luck. Maxine had dumped him when he refused to get behind her on the help Shondrella escape plan. Ali said he felt it was best if he just stayed away from the situation all together. He admitted that he loved Maxine very much. Ali knew they both needed help and they were in constant denial and refused his many offers. He knew if he hung around, he would end up crazy himself or locked up from some foolery they caused. Ali was adamant and firm on his decision, he filed for divorce wanting no more ties to Maxine. Ralph understood and let him know there were no hard feelings between the two of them. "FUCK!" Ralph cursed to himself as he released his sister. The nurse gave her something to sedate her because she would not calm down. He stepped into the hallway to see his goons talking to Slick Rick. "This can't be good", he thought as he approached them. Rick led them to a small conference room and began to tell them everything that was going on. Ralph immediately called Donald, even if he denied involvement with his niece, he and his family deserved to know what was going on with the whole ordeal.

Donald and Big C arrived at the hospital in record time. Neither of them said a word on the ride over, just thinking about how this mess could all be over and soon. Donald sent a text to Ralph letting him know they were there. Not wanting to cause confusion, Ralph met with them outside so they could talk freely and away from nosey people. Ralph told them everything that Rick had explained to him, including their involvement with the situation. "Before you protest or lie to me, DON'T! It is insulting. Besides, I do not really blame you for your actions, but I wish you would have come to me first because now I must deal with my sister and her possible mental breakdown", Ralph stated firmly. He wanted to be pissed but he knew firsthand how shit goes in the streets. Ralph felt so bad especially after hearing everything what Shondrella had done to them and others in this short period of time. "From here on out you have to listen to me so that we can keep this shit show as clean as possible". Big C agreed, Donald just looked at him like he was waiting for the rest of the conversation. Ralph continued. "Since Clifton is awake, and by some miracle he is mentally more stable now than he was prior to the shooting, he will be a witness against Shondrella". 'He has given his statement willingly to the FBI and local police who are standing guard at Shondrella's door, so you don't have to worry about her coming after you even if she pulls through her injuries". Ralph took a deep breath and pulled out some rolling papers. "Deuce is having his dick reattached, I do not know what to say about that". Ralph fires up the joint "That was crazy as fuck to hear about, and I can only imagine the pain", Ralph grabbed his dick absentmindedly. "Shit was crazier to see", Big C laughed, reaching for the joint. "I had my people go back and destroy the shallow grave my niece was found in". Donald and Big C nodded in appreciation, "No need to have this fuck with your lives even more, what's done is done". Hopefully, shit can go back to normal after this". "Hell yeah", they agreed.

Just then Ralph's phone began to ring as well as Donald's. Walking off in two different directions answering their phones, Big C took the time to call her sister to check on her. She had been doing a lot of thinking since they left the house, and she was going to help Courtney and Donald no matter how stubborn they both were. She helped Donald plan the best makeup I love you weekend, they both knew it had to be over the top. All Big C had to do was get Courtney there. She was going to do one better and get her there sexy and ready to rumble. If anyone deserved to be together it was Courtney and Donald, and she was ready to rekindle the fire. After getting off the phone with her sister Big C went in search for Donald. When she walked inside the hospital, all hell had broken loose. Shondrella was awake and snitching like a bitch. Ralph was doing as much damage control as possible. He pulled Dr. Racqi to the side and informed him that he knew about he and his wife fuck encounters with his niece and all the other shady shit that was going on. Ralph flashed the paperwork that was proof and looked at the Dr. with much shame. "The medical board will have a field day with this one, "don't you agree"? "What do you want me to do?" Dr. Racqi asked "I need you to lie, you are no stranger in that area". "Tell the authorities that Shondrella is suffering from something only you would understand". "Make this shit look good; I would hate for your colleagues and the local news to know how you and your wife both were fucking and taking complete advantage of a mental patient". "Push the fact that she's out of her mind and more delusional and incoherent than before". "We need her statements to be discredited, make that happen NOW". Maxine overheard him and she went ballistic. She could not believe that her brother was betraying her like this. She began rocking back and forth. She was not thinking straight. "They all have to pay", she said repeatedly to herself.

Big C caught up to Karizma in the coffee shop, where they were just talking about the current situation at hand. Karizma let Big C know that she would be taking over Deuce's operation "If you want in Bitch, holla at a Boss". Ya feel me", she laughed and high fived Big C. "A pimp with no dick, where they do that at?" "You know I'm pancakes and your waffle's and we both add sweetness and flavor count me in, I want to wear big panties too". The girls continued to laugh, catching up on old times.

The staff worked hard to get Shondrella stabilized, now the FBI is taking her back to their facility to face her crimes. She will be held in the infirmary until she recovers completely. Shondrella breaks down crying, giving the biggest pity party. She yells out telling her mom and the staff that she is sorry; begging and pleading to Maxine for her not let them take her. Maxine has this what can I do look on her face. Shondrella then screams so loud that spits fly out her mouth; she is telling her mom "Bitch you don't care about me, you down with these cracker mutha fuckas", "ok bitch play wit it". "I will kill myself this time and haunt you from the grave". She continued to scream and fight as they begin to strap her to the gurney to prevent her from moving. "The nurse yells for security, they need help, Shondrella's moving was becoming too much. The nurse grabs a syringe trying to sedate her. Shondrella being quick on her feet she snatched the syringe and stabbed it into her heart giving it a twist and turn. She was already highly medicated, so added medication to her heart took effect instantly. She was dead Within minutes. It was a horrific scene that could definitely be used in a horror movie for sure. Maxine dropped her head, and a devilish grin was plastered across her face, she slow walked out the hospital while biting her nails. Maxine's body begins to twitch, and tears rolled down her face, she was numb and full of pain. She had a high tolerance for revenge, "If they think Shondrella was crazy these mutha fuckars haven't seen shit yet". That is what Maxine said in a low tone as she proceeded to walk away.

Chapter 18

MAKING UP IS HARD TO DO

TONIGHT, WAS THE BIG extravaganza that Donald had planned for Courtney. Courtney tried to shake off the fact that Donald questioned her loyalty; she had been staying at Sabrina's house teaching Donald a lesson. So, all the sisters decided to follow her and stayed there as well, taring Sabrina's nerves up. Sabrina wanted all their asses to go home, her and her man Terrence who she calls Daddy T could not get their freak on with her daughters lingering around. Sabrina loved her kids unconditionally, but she loved getting some dick just as much as them. Donald had his art gallery furnished with wall size portraits of Courtney all over. The light that shinned down across the portraits gave them an extra glow. The gallery was laced in silver and black décor, trimmed in diamonds. The candles were six feet tall lined across the walls, the scenery spoke grown and sexy fit for a true Queen Bean Diva. There was a live band playing all of Courtney favorites from her personal playlist. Food was catered from her favorite restaurant Crabs or us. Sabrina's boyfriend Daddy T had the bar jumping with drinks. Two celebrity guests were waiting for their cue to come out. The gallery was turned into a palace. Donald was headed in the right direction to get back in Courtney's good grace. Sabrina along with the sisters managed to get Courtney out the house, they had done a day of beauty treatments hair, nails, make-up they all were looking HOLLYWOOD. Not wanting to give too much detail away, so their clothes were at the gallery. Courtney had a short silver and diamond dress that would complement her hair and make-up so well. Arriving at the gallery Courtney turns her nose up and asks, "what the fuck we are doing her for Ma"? "Girl, watch your damn mouth and get your narrow ass out this car". "Let us go in and see what your man got going on", I know your pussy hot, and need some touch and feels come let Donald take care of that and take your ass back home". Everybody was out the car but Courtney, Sabrina started counting 1 2 3, Courtney rushed out the car to join her sisters. She had a flash back from growing up when Sabrina did the countdown somebody was about to get their ass whipped. As they walked in the gallery there were ushers lined up at the door with their clothing attire in hand. Big C grabbed her clothes then ask one of the ushers for some pineapple Ciroc. Courtney was blushing and she begin to feel happy, but she kept a mean mug on her face trying to keep up her mad image. They all made b line to the dressing area, Courtney just teared up after seeing her dress, she remembered telling Donald she wanted to where this exact dress after they were married for their reception. "One of y'all hoes tell me what's going on"? Courtney said out loud to all the sisters. Caz responded "just lay back kick it and enjoy the ride", singing one of Xscapes oldies. "Beauty talk to me give me a heads up or something". "Sorry sis Big C will cut me if I talk". Just then Big C walks in "stop trying to pick Beauty, get dress sis and come on out". Big C gave Courtney a kiss on the check and said, "I love you, we all just want you to be the queen you are for tonight". The sisters entered the gallery first, moments later Courtney walks in looking breath taking. The gallery was packed with family and friends. One more chance by Biggie was playing loudly through the speakers, Faith Evans herself was at a table off to the side singing the hook live. Courtney's smile was to the roof when she notices all her college sorrows and family, she was extra excited to see her all time bestie Bella, whom she has not seen in a while. Courtney begins to jump up and down once she seen Faith Evans get out her seat and walk toward her singing. Faith grabbed her hand and started singing "please give Donald one more chance" she added that to the hook killing the verse. All Courtney could do was smile; she was at a loss for words. She did not see Donald nowhere in sight she was ready to forgive him, her love came raining down on her she was feeling like a schoolgirl with a crush. The night continued dancing, drinking, photoshoots, the party was lit. Courtney was having so much fun, but she had yet to see Donald. "Hey baby now aren't you glad you got your ass out that car said Sabrina". "yes ma'am, ma why haven't I seen Donald"? I need to talk with him". "I don't know, he should be here somewhere just keep enjoying yourself". Courtney took her mom's advice and let loose she danced the night away with her sisters and friends, they all flooded social media with pictures and posts from the party. The DJ calls Courtney to the front that was every bodies cue. The lights went dim all the guest moved to the side and held up signs that read different quotes from I love you to please forgive me. Music starts to play then the group Jagged Edge walks in singing their hit song Let's get married, followed close behind the group was Donald. Jagged Edge serenades her. Halfway through the song they move to the side and there was Donald in an all-white Armani suit down on one knee with three dozen of roses and a rock that would break your arm. Donald had upgraded Courtney's ring to a 4 karat round diamond band laced with mad diamonds. Donald poured his heart out for forgiveness, but before he could finish Courtney passes her roses to Sabrina and she kisses Donald like they were about to have sex on the gallery floor. The two moved to a private area and Donald had one more surprise. He booked a flight and arranged for them to get married in Hawaii tomorrow. The flight was set to leave at 12 mid-night. "Please grant me this wish, I know you were stuck on February I really don't want to crush your childhood dream, but I can't wait any longer". "What are we going to do about packing "? Was Courtney's response. "Dacember and Beauty already packed all that you will need". "you know you are my Queen Bean, it's like I been fighting to keep you I want you to become Mrs. Donald Murphy tomorrow". "Shit has been crazy lately for both of us, I love you is an understatement; I adore you and cherish you". Please forgive me I will never let you down or shame you again". "Nigga you are lucky I seen Jagged Edge and I got a full photo shoot with Faith Evans; I was going to make you wait a whole year before I gave in". "Yeah, right you would have been begging daddy by next week for some dick who you think your fooling". They continued to talk and make out; then Donald picked Courtney up and carried her to the limo they headed home to gather their luggage and off to Hawaii they went.

Chapter 19

THIS SHIT HAS TO END

ALI FELT LIKE HE owed Donald and Courtney a warning about Maxine. He knew deep down it was going to be some shit. He pulls up at their crib unexpected. After ringing the doorbell Daddy T answers, with a what the fuck you want look on his face. Sabrina was seconds behind him. "Can I help you" Sabrina asks with much attitude. "Yes, ma'am I'm sorry to bother you, but is Donald or Courtney here by any chance"? "NO, THEY ARE NOT"." WHO THE FUCK ARE YOU; AND WHAT THE FUCK YOU WANT WITH MY DAUGHTER"? "I'm not here for any trouble by far I just want to pass along that my soon to be ex-wife Maxine may try to revenge her daughter's death and cause trouble for them two". "I only wanted to warn them because she is very unstable that's why I'm divorcing her". "I am Sabrina Courtney's mother, let me tell you something Mr. soon to be ex-husband". "If that coo-coo bird dumb nut bucket ass bitch come anywhere near my child I will fuck her up with no Vaseline, I advise you to make sure her insurance policy is active before you divorce her; you can be a rich man, because I'm subject to kill that bitch". "I do not play the radio when it comes to my kids". "Yes, ma'am I agree 100%". "Just have them check their surroundings and be cautious". "Thanks for the heads up I will be sure to pass it along". Sabrina was now mad as hell. Her daughter had been through hell and she will not allow Shondrella's mom to torment her to. "These hoes bloodline is damaged, the damn mama nuts too". Sabrina was venting to Daddy T. "Don't worry baby we will protect our brand by any means necessary, no need to bother Donald and Courtney at this point". Sabrina and Daddy T was house sitting while they were away. Sabrina calls Big C and give her the run down on the situation, Big C then calls Caz on three way so they both could hear the tea. After the call Big C called Tuesday and Cotton and Karizma over along with BG. After everyone arrived and got settled in, they hear somebody walk through the door they all reach for their firearm. Then walks in Sabrina. "Y'all mutha fuckas too damn slow I would have been dropped at least three of y'all". "Ma what are you doing over here". "I raised you, so I know how you think". "You got something in the mix, and I want in, and your sisters on their way too". At this point everybody was ready for war. Sabrina being the most aggressive and violent one. The sisters looking totally confused, they knew their mom was crazy and would fuck them up from time to time but the shit she was talking was extra extraordinary for them. Sabrina spoke on some assassination military brutal events. They hoped that this lady came to her senses because clearly Maxine do not want any smoke from Sabrina. Big C looked at all her sisters and said, "but y'all say I'm the crazy one". Daddy T decides to get shit poppin by having a sit down with Ralph. The meet was taking place at Ralph's law firm. Daddy T walks in and was greeting by the nice secretary, she kindly said right this way Sir Mr. Ralph is expecting you. The men shook hands, once they were seated Ralph said, "what's the urgency of this meeting". Daddy T exhaled then spoke, "We both know shit has been weird and crazy for both sides of the family circle". "I just want to ask you not to help your sister do anything stupid against my family". "We both know she's going to try something". "I agree I love my sister very much but at this point after losing my niece and fighting to save them both for so many years, I'm at a halt with that mess". "I'm going to end up losing my wife if I don't get a grip of shit ". "I don't want to see her hurt or dead, but I can't save crazy, I promised my wife that no matter how much she begs I will stay out of it, and that's what I'm doing". "I would like to thank you for that I know you are a man with much power, but my family has suffered enough". "I will say this, I tried to have Maxine committed but the state disagreed with me". "A valuable word of advice, if she comes for your family, on GOD I hate to say this; but the only way your family will be at piece is to eliminate her or she's going to keep coming back". Ralph was in tears by the end of the conversation, but he knew his sister all so well. Maxine had started her part 1 of her plan. She needed to be able to move around without being spotted. Maxine cut off all her hair put on a pair of store-bought glasses. She then purchased a fat suit. The suit was used for personal trainers to let their clients know how it feels to be overweight. With this suit on she looked like an average bald fat woman, professor Klump would describe it best. She spent the day purchasing a series of items one being a gun from the pawn shop. Ralph had notified all pawn shops to alert him if a Maxine Hicks-Blackwell comes in a buy a firearm. He was alerted through a text, but his wife intercepted and did not respond or did she tell him about it. Maxine makes her way to Donald and Courtney's home. Maxine spots an Amazon driver doing deliveries. When the driver guy makes his way to the consumers porch and place the package on the front doorstep, she sneaks in the inside of the van. When the driver returned, he gets in to proceed to his next destination, but before he could take off Maxine comes from the back pointing her gun, placing it directly against his head. She asks the man "what is your name"? He says "Brian". "Well Brian I am not going to hurt you I promise". "I just need you to drive me around and do what I say". "Will you be able to follow those instructions Brian"? "Yes, ma'am PLEASE DO NOT HURT ME I have kids" the skinny white man begs Maxine with teary eyes. "Just relax and drive I will keep my word you will not be harmed, just don't try anything act like were old friends". The driver gave her a look of disgust before pulling off. Maxine instructs Brian to park directly across the street from Donald's house. Maxine observed the house for hours, Brian spoke up "we are going to raise a red flag if we continue to sit here". "I need to keep my eyes on this house it's very important, so what do you suggest I do, moving this van is not an option". "I have a video doorbell camera in the back that needs to be delivered in another area, but I can camouflage the camera in the flower arrangement on the porch". "That way you can watch from blocks over, the camera will pick up on the WIFI in the neighborhood once I link it to my phone". "Awesome sauce" Maxine blurts out. While Brian was off playing inspector gadget Maxine helped herself to some more items he had in the back of the van. Brian returned and assured her no one was there now". Maxine took the keys out of the ignition and told Brian to follow her. They both are walking through the yard looking for a way in. Maxine notices a small crack in a window at least 10 feet high up. Maxine looks at Brian and tells him to climb up and go through the window then open the door once he gets in. Brian did not exchange no words he just did what she said, he struggled to climb up the side of the house to raise the window up. Luckily, he was not spotted. Finally, he opened the door and Maxine immediately starts snooping around she sees luggage on the floor in the upstairs bedroom she takes out some itch powder from her bag that she stole out of the van. She takes her time and rub it in the seat of Sabrina's underwear. She moves to the kitchen and does the unthinkable, she pisses in the orange juice container then wipe her ass with the sandwich meat. Maxine tells Brian, "I'm going to bend over, and I need for you to stick this wooden spoon up my ass far as you can". "I need to be able to shit so I can leave them a nice little surprise in this left-over spaghetti". Maxine bent over and spreded her ass checks; Brain said, "are you serious ma'am". "As a heart attack". Brian frowned up and he used that as an opportunity to cause her some pain so he shoved the spoon hard as he could in her ass". She got what she wanted a pan full of shit. She must be satisfied with the results because she smiled as she walked out the door with a shitty ass. Brian was steps behind her wondering what the fuck these people had done to her, and if he had some sanitizer wipes in the back of the van so she could wipe her shitty ass,

Chapter 20

THE DOCTOR'S ORDER

DEUCE MAGIC STICK WAS able to be saved but he could not reach the full capacity of an erection. He was devastated about that. The field he was in he often was friendly with his man part, he fucked like a porn star with multiple bitches. Deuce use to put the spread on thick like Jiffy peanut butter. The party may be over because getting some pussy with a limp noodle is not much excitement for the ladies. Deuce made it official that Karizma was the one who would be running shit. Deuce calls up Karizma and tells her to have Blossom pack her shit and come to his new spot with him. He was about to settle down with blossom and try out his new equipment, he had hyped himself up by saying it is not the size of the dick it is the motion you put in the ocean. He felt if his back was strong, he was still able to shut the sex game down. Karizma had to prove herself on her first day in action as the boss. After delivering the message to Blossom, Blossom refused her request. "Wait a minute bitch this is not optional this is a mutha fuckan demand so, just like my girl Jasmine Sullivan says you got 10 seconds to put some fire to your ass and bust a move". "I'm not about to be tied down with Deuce with that cut off dick, when all these ballers out here paying and slaying". Blossom smacked her lips and rolled her eyes after she was done speaking. Karizma gives Blossom a two-piece combo with a biscuit punching her directly in the face, followed by a double smack that caused her face to shift. Blossom nose was broken, blood was everywhere within in seconds. "What you not going to do is disrespect me like I'm not the boss, you're going to do exactly what I said", and just for the disrespect you will not work the set anymore"." You will be

Deuce personal fuck doll". "Now you can clean yourself up and be on your way". Slick Rick will put your nose back together and give him some head for his service, not that mediocre shit make it sloppy". "Be nice and Show some compassion for my boss; stop and get Deuce some balloons and his favorite strawberry cake with the cookie filling". "One more thing, be sure to grab some lube since his dick is broken, I'm sure he will be putting something in that ass". Karizma walks out feeling just like the head bitch in charge, she hears Blossom screaming from Rick jamming her nose back in place. On her way to meet up with Big C she makes a stop at Clifton's new group home. Speaking with management she lays the law down that Clifton is to be taking care of, and at least once a week he was to get a supervised visit at one of her spots so he can get his fuck on. She hands over a large amount of cash to the manger on duty. The man smiled and agreed to all the terms. Daddy T was taken Sabrina out to dinner at Ruth's Chris steak house. Sabrina showered then got dressed she was looking sexy Daddy T could not stop touching her. They arrived at the restaurant and Daddy T notices that Sabrina was being squirmy as they walked inside. "You good bae Daddy T asks Sabrina". "Yes, I'm straight these shoes are new, and they are a bit tight I have to break them in". "OK you are looking uncomfortable, just had to check". They were seated and ordered their food while waiting they had a few drinks and engaged in some sex talk, the two got so deep the waitress started to ear hustle. Sabrina starts to become itchy in her vagina area, she did some secrets move to try to hide the fact that her pussy was itching. She excused herself to the rest room once she entered the stall, she scratched her pussy like she had crabs. She wet some paper towels with cool water then wiped her pussy aggressively up and down to soothe the itch. Sabrina made her way back to the table and there was no way she could sit through dinner. Sabrina returned to the table and said, "Terrence suddenly I'm not feeling well let's get our food to go". "Sure, thing bae I will go notify our waitress". Daddy T knew something was wrong because Sabrina never calls him Terrence. During the ride home Daddy T makes conversation trying to get Sabrina to tell him something. "Sabrina talk to me what the fuck is up, your all fidgety you spent over 30 minutes in the restroom, then you suddenly gets sick". "Since you must know nigga, I'm having some feminine issues my pussy itching like a mutha fucka, I'm about to scratch a new hole down there". "I think I'm having an allergic reaction to Courtney's soap she had in the shower". "Take me back to the house so I can shower again, then take me to the Emergency Center". Sabrina took a hot shower not using no soap on her vagina, she dries off putting on a fresh pair of underwear out of her suitcase. Driving to their destination Sabrina was scratching so hard Daddy T told started to itch. "Lighten up bae you're going to harm that pussy you know I'm addicted to that shit you carry around". Sabrina gave him a dirty look then yelled, "Hurry up, drive this mutha fuckan car nigga"! Soon as Daddy T pulls up to the front of the Emergency Center Sabrina jumps out the car. Sabrina speed walks in and tells the triage nurse she needs a rag and some cool water for her vagina. "I can take you straight back but I need to get your name so I can place a bracelet on your arm the nurse explained". "Yes, ma'am please hurry". Sabrina wasted no time telling the nurse what she had been experiencing. "I'm nurse Abby follow me to room 5, I will need you take off all your clothes". "I will get the Doctor in here soon as possible". Sabrina took off all her clothes as instructed she then wipe between her legs with cool water and rag, she places the gown on that was folded on the bed. Daddy T walks in and take a seat seconds later the doctor comes in. "Hello Ms. Wilks, I am Dr. Bentley I hear you are having some itch problems". Sabrina goes into details telling the doctor basically the same story she told the nurse. "I would like to examine your vagina area and see if I see anything abnormal". "Also, I need to eliminate the possibility of you being allergic to cotton or lace, or maybe even the detergent, so I will be taking a culture of your underwear as well". After the examination Sabrina realize the itching has stopped without her clothes on. One hour later Dr. Bentley comes in with lab results, Ms. Wilks your labs show you had a heavy amount of itch powder in the seat of your underwear, that's what was causing the itching". "Your vagina is squeaky clean no bacteria or yeast". "It was the itch powder indeed". "How the fuck some itch powder gets in my damn underwear, OMG this is crazy". "I suggest when you purchase underwear from now on make sure you wash them first". "I will make sure I do so, but I have worn these undies and the ones I had on before these plenty of times so this had to be deliberately done". "Thanks Doc lets go Daddy T". Sabrina storms out the Emergency Center with just the gown on leaving her clothes behind, she was quiet as a mouse during the ride. Her mind was doing cartwheels trying to figure this shit out. When Sabrina and Daddy T arrive back at Courtney and Donald's house, they both walk around casing the place looking for anything strange. Just as Sabrina looks up, she notices the window at the top was all the way up. "Look at this shit Daddy T, that window was not like that I specifically had a small crack in that window Sabrina blurts out". "Daddy T pulls out his 45 and open the door they look all over the place, Sabrina cell phone rings and it was Courtney. "Sabrina answers the phone clearing her nerves and anger. "Hey baby girl how is the married life and Hawaii treating you". "I am so happy Mommy; Donald will not let me lift a finger". "That's awesome I want you to relax and have fun and drink plenty of water so my Grandson can be healthy". "Now what if it's a girl". "well, she needs to be healthy too, after raising 7 girls I'm team boy". "How are things coming along with you and Daddy T house sitting, I know y'all are being some big freaks". They chopped it up for a few more minutes, then Courtney added. "You can download the camera to your phone if you want to stay home a few nights". "what camera Sabrina ask"? "Donald and I installed a camera when shit was crazy around there, the main box is beside the fireplace the directions are on the panel". "OK love you enjoy the rest of your honeymoon, I love you sweetness". "I love you more Mommy". They ended the call. Daddy T overheard the conversation he was already gathering the device he rewinds the video footage, and boom he see Maxine and the Amazon driver in the house. When Sabrina joined in, they both seen Maxine in Sabrina's suitcase placing the itch powder in her panties. Adding insult to injury they witness Maxine wipe her ass with the cold cuts they just made a sandwich with earlier that day, they both could not believe what they were seeing when Brian put the spoon up Maxine's ass. Daddy T rushes to the bathroom and vomit all over the floor. Sabrina just stared at the rest of the video with a devilish grin on her face she finally turned it off and said to herself, "GAME ON BITCH, IM ABOUT TO GIVE YOU EXACTLY WHAT YOU WANT"!

Chapter 21

THE BATTLE BRAWL

KARIZMA WAS OUT DOING rounds, her first stop was with Lucy at the Quake Shack. Lucy always kept shit together on her end. Lucy defiantly kept twelve away, and chin checked all the out of line crack heads. Even without Slick Rick around shit was still running smoothly. Lucy greets Karizma with a bow then says, "what's up boss lady"? "Cut it out I'm the same person I'll never switch up on my fam". "The boss look fits you good, you glowing and shit". "bitch I been a boss in these streets you better google me, besides that's what healthy dick and unlimited head do to you". "OK I see you been getting your back blowed out by that young nigga Surge". "Mind ya business hoe". Karizma said while she playfully hit Lucy on the arm. "Since you put it that way maybe we can collaborate on this situation I'm in". "Talk to me what's up"? "Well, you know I have been helping Trixie out, giving her a hide out because she hot right now due to the bank robberies". "Yes, I had kind of forgot about that". "You know we was about to do trap the robberies on the crazy bitch before shit went left and she killed herself". "Long story short fam; I need help getting her some plastic surgery because she can't keep hiding out". "Right now, I have her tucked away, but we both know shit don't last forever". "Her and I are pretty much a couple now, it went from me helping her hide out, to me on top of her". "What the fuck you a carpet muncher now"? You went from sucking dicks to sucking pussy, got to be more careful". "But I aint the one to judge, just keep her out of sight for a few more weeks while I set things up with my folks". "You sure you want to get all the way deep with this chic like that, aint no turning back once you put the cuffs on her". "She good fam, I got this". "Well, this shit going to cost her; I'm not working pro bono so tell her to hold on to that cheese real tight". "Thanks, so much Karizma I knew I could count on you". Its all-good fam you keep shit flowing for us, so one favor deserves another". Big C was hanging close to Sabrina after Daddy T gave her the scoop on what went down. "Big C I don't know why you insist on following my every move, I do not need no damn babysitter Sabrina says loudly". "Ma, people got our family twisted, I hurt people for fun so imagine what I will do if a mutha fucka cross the line with my Ma Dukes". Sabrina walks up to Big C and smack her face "watch your mouth Chelsea". The rest of the sisters laughed at Big C, she responded by sticking her middle finger up at them, then dropped her head like a five-year-old kid. Daddy T wanted to in lighten the mood, so he did what black folks do best, he pulled out the grill since everybody was over. He told the girls "if y'all gather the food and stuff together I will do all the cooking". Big C calls up BG and the rest of the crew to join the festivities. Sabrina remembered there was no barbeque sauce or paper plates. "I got to make a quick run to the store", before she could even finish her sentence all the sisters jumped up at said we are going too. Sabrina shook her head and they all piled in Daddy T Cadillac. Along the ride to the store, a few blocks over they notice the Amazon van they spotted a ball headed lady that fits the description of Maxine hop in the back. Sabrina pulls away from the fan she instructs the girls to creep up slowly. Sabrina grabs her brass knuckles out of her purse she places her hunting knife in her bra. Once they were at the back of the van Caz tapped on the door softly. Maxine must have thought a neighbor was asking about a package because they had someone do that earlier. Soon as Maxine opens the van door Sabrina grabbed her out the back and slammed her hard down on the ground. Big C, Z.Z. and Caz see Maxine reach for a gun, and they immediately take it from her. Sabrina said "y'all back up I got this one". Sabrina stomps Maxine repeatedly in the face, taking her leg all the back and coming forward with forceful kicks. Maxine grabs Sabrina's leg and pulls herself up, Maxine tried to swing but Sabrina did not give her a chance. Sabrina then starts to punch her blow after blow, right then left punches all to the face with the brass knuckles making the punches more deadly. Maxine starts to stumble her face was bleeding profusely. Maxine was not able to even pinch Sabrina. Sabrina was not letting up, "You stanking ugly ass bitch you keep fucking with my family about your looney ass daughter, fuck you and that bitch I'm glad the hoe dead". Sabrina was still swinging but she was wearing out. Sabrina was going ham; her daughters could not believe their eyes. Right before Sabrina could get her knife out to dissect Maxine the girls put Sabrina back in the car; then threw Maxine back in the van headfirst. Nobody noticed the driver the whole time, he was shaking in his boots. When he seen the girls come his way, he threw his hands up in the surrender position. Caz said to him. "We know you are innocent in this, but we need for you to drop her off at this address". Caz got paper and pen out of Sabrina's purse and gave him Ralph's law firm address. "just drop her ass off and keep going; understood". Brian responded "Yes Ma'am" with a crackling voice. Ralph was on the golf course with some of his colleagues when he received a phone call from one of his men Clarence. Thirty minutes into the phone call Ralph hangs up the phone. Clarence had taken Maxine to the Emergency Center once he found her in that condition. He stayed there out of respect for his boss. Clarence did not want to leave her alone, but at the same time he was feeling uncomfortable with the police asking him questions. They were drilling him like this was a domestic violence case. Ralph arrives and his wife Monica was glued to his hills, she was even mad that he came to see about her. "Ralph don't get in here with that sentimental shit, you can't save that hoe, you see you couldn't save the damn daughter either". Monica was fed up and did not give two fucks what was wrong with Maxine. The doctor came out after Maxine was cleaned up, he alarmed Ralph that Maxine suffered some serious face injuries. She had a few missing teeth, and her mouth will be temporarily wired. She would be admitted for at least a week depending on how fast she recovers. "The bitch just like a cat she got nine lives, let's go Ralph aint shit you can do". Monica said with much attitude. Monica then turns to the Doctor and said, "my husband is not to be bothered with any decision-making questions when it comes to Maxine Hicks-Blackwell". "She is a full-grown woman, and she can stand on her own two feet, from this moment on my husband needs to be on the do not disturb list". "My organization gives good money to this hospital yearly; I would hate to take the funds to another hospital". Maxine spoke very intelligently and stern. Ralph stood there as if he was in trouble at the principal's office not uttering a word. Ralph slipped Clarence some money and he automatically knew to leave it with Maxine's belongings. Karizma had placed a 911 call to Dr. Racqi and Debbie. They spoke briefly on the phone only about a location where to meet. Deciding on Chucky Cheese that will be the one place no one would be at 12 noon. When Racqi and Debbie walks in the table was fully loaded with pizza, salads and drinks.

"I know you Doctors never have time to eat so help yourself". "They both looked amazed at the food and it did not take long before the two-dug in. "So, we both know this is not just a pizza party so what's the verdict", Dr. Racqi spoke up first. "You both know when I come, I have a money proposition". "Keep talking, said Debbie. "I have a female that is running from the law and she needs plastic surgery". "Wow how the fuck we suppose to pull that off in a public hospital?" Racqi said with a mouth full of pizza. "I guess how you two being doing mischievous shit all along, this is nothing out the norm compared to the business we have done in the past". "What's the ticket Racqi ask". "Half a million, but the money must be washed it's from a bank robbery". Silence was at the table for several minutes while everyone continued to eat. Debbie broke the silence first and said I'm in". Racqi gave a thumbs up while drinking his soda from a straw. "Cool, once you two come up with a game plan with a date and time let me know in advance and your money will be left at the usual drop off spot Karizma said as she grabbed another slice of pizza then walked out.

Chapter 22

TAKE ME AWAY

MEANWHILE DONALD AND COURTNEY were living their best life starting out as husband and wife, having their dream come true in Hawaii. They were down to two more days of enjoyment. Donald was the perfect gentlemen; Courtney was getting foot rubs, back massages and kept his tongue in her pussy. Donald catered to her every need. Alvin was able to sneak in an adventurous boat ride as a wedding gift from him. They were notified from front desk that there was a mystery surprise waiting for them. They both were curious, so Donald scheduled for the limo to pick them up after brunch. There was a clue for them to wear swim wear, so they gathered their attire and headed for the limo. The limo had Donald's favorite liquor Crown ready for him to drink. Courtney had juices and enough fruit to supply a village. The chocolate covered strawberries and miniature cheesecake bites were displayed so beautifully. Bryson Tiller was pumping through the speakers. A flat screen monitor slides down inside of the limo from the top of the roof. On the monitor there was Alvin via face time, "Hello my awesome family". "What's up bro"? "So, you are the one responsible for this ride along I see". "Hey brother-in-law, Courtney says aloud". "Hello sis", "I could not let you two come all the way back to South Carolina without giving you a proper wedding gift". "We greatly appreciate your act of kindness bro". "You guys have fun and take care of my nephew". "There you go so I see you team boy too huh". "Most defiantly us Murphy men or rare form". "See you guys when y'all touch down". A few moments after the video ended the driver comes to a halt. He walks around to open the door for them to exit. The driver shows them the direction they needed to go. They both walk off proudly feeling important. Moving along swiftly holding hands and anxious at the same time. Two Hawaiian men approach them with a hammock. The men explained that it was traditional for the bride to be carried. Courtney was placed on the hammock and they continue to walk. Donald was so close to Courtney he felt weary of the men carrying his wife, he kept side eying the two men. They arrived on a beach that was downright gorgeous. Donald and Courtney being the only two on the entire beach besides the driver and staff. The water was so clear and blue, the décor was over the top sheers hanging from bamboo poles and flowing with the wind. The same set up from the limo was immaculate laid oud for them on the beach table. "OMG bae this is to die for Courtney said as she starts to cry". "Donald said I agree". Donald picks Courtney up and carry her out deep down the beach shore, he places her down and just held her so tight. These two were so in love, they had a vibrant connection. Sparks was flying through their body the two was about to bust with sexual emotions. Donald made passionate love to his wife on the beach on top of the sand, that was a scene only lovers could create. After hours of love making and enjoying each other sexually and fulfilling each other needs, the two stood up and was about to walk the beach. Just then a yacht boat appears up on the shore with the name Murphy on the side. "Shit just keep getting better" Courtney said as she grabbed her belongings and heads to the boat with a Christmas day smile. They continued the adventure on the yacht doing all kind of fun things. They danced, did karaoke, played shuffleboard. They took several pictures and videos. Courtney posted them to their IG tagging Alvin giving him a big shot out. They ate so many crab legs the ocean may need to be replenished. There was a personal masseuse and they both felt like they were in heaven from the full body massage. The day ended by them relaxing in the hot tub under each other, they both drifted off to sleep tired from the long day of activities. Their day was completely amazing. The next day Courtney continued to get special treatment from Donald she started out with a pancake breakfast in bed. Donald had scheduled a visit with a Hawaiian OBGYN Doctor. Courtney was now 14 weeks and her babies' gender was about to be revealed. They were going to keep the envelope closed and find out when they reveal the news to everyone back home. During the ultrasound

Courtney immediately felt a connection, she was convinced it was a girl. The newlyweds plus parents to be became emotional when they heard their baby's heartbeat. When they left the Doctor's office Donald was all smiles. "I Would love for you to give me a son, but I know my daughter would be as pretty as you, my feeling would not be hurt if it's a girl". The two went back to their room getting ready to say good-bye to Hawaii their flight was scheduled to leave at 5 am, after packing their luggage they decided to rest up for their early morning flight. Courtney had managed to call Beauty and Bonnie; she gave them the run down on her ultrasound and how she was going to share the news with the family regarding the gender when Donald and she returned home. Beauty and Bonnie decided to give Courtney a gender reveal shower. They spent Two hours on the phone giving all the sisters and family on both sides the information and making plans altogether. Donald's mom Vernetta was an interior decorator and party coordinator, so she oversaw that. Sabrina and Daddy T were both grill masters so that is where they fit in. Everybody else was to be there putting things in place making the event nice. They decided on Donald and Courtney's house for the location, now that the two deranged stalkers are out the way things are smooth sailing. Maxine was trying to rush her recovery she was 75% better, but she still needed care. Her being the person she is she was looking for a way out she helped Shondrella escape from a lot worse places than an Emergency Center. She was very observant and planned to make a run for it during 3rd shift. After nurse Karen did her rounds, she would talk on her phone most of the night to her boyfriend and nothing else seemed to exist during her call. That was going to be the distraction Maxine needed. Maxine played it cool all the way up until shift change soon as nurse Karen made her rounds and propped her feet on the desk, Maxine smiled and proceeded with her plan. Maxine had tied a t-shirt around her head wearing it as scarf she had purchased her some pajamas from the gift shop with the money Ralph left her. She did not look to much like a patient she just needed to dodge security, she knew they could not do nothing to her. Maxine did not want the hassle of them trying to make her stay. The escape was easy breezy Maxine had made her way to the lobby and walk clean out the door without anyone noticing her. Nurse Karen did not realize Maxine was gone until shift change the next morning at 7am. She walked all over the hospital. She checked floor after floor before she notified Beth the 1st shift supervisor that Maxine was missing. After talking to Beth, Beth told her there was nothing the hospital could do unless she was court ordered, the hospital could not hold her against her will. Beth then turns the heat on her and ask, "what were you doing so important you didn't see Ms. Hicks leave"? Karen did not have an answer or explanation, all she provided was a shit face look. Beth then told her to clean out her locker she was fired. The hospital did not follow Monica orders, they placed a call to Ralph alerting him his sister had left on her own will, Monica heard the call and rolled her eyes then turned back over in bed. When Monica got up to get her day started, she got dressed and she skipped breakfast. Monica told Ralph she had some errands to run, and she would not be gone long. Monica pulls up at Courtney and Donald's house. Monica rings the doorbell, Sabrina answers seconds later with a spatula in her hand she was cooking breakfast. Monica stated who she was, and Sabrina instantly started going in "why the fuck y'all family can't stay the fuck away from us"? Monica said, "chill I know your frustration but I'm on your side trust me". "That bitch Maxine left the hospital and I know she is up to no good". "She is going to target your family and cause trouble every chance she gets". "Woman to woman I been in that family a long time and my husband and I have been through the ringer with the mother daughter psychopaths". "I can't stand the bitch and I will give my right arm for her to disappear". I'm going to leave you with this, these ass whippings you are dishing out not going to cut it with this bitch". The only way and I repeat the only way to get rid of her for good is to send her daughter some company". Sabrina looked at her and said, "I don't want no problems out of your husband when I off this bitch". "You leave my husband to me, I got that". Sabrina extended her hand for a friendly shake then said, "say less".

Chapter 23

CRAZY AND DERANGED

THE FAMILY START TO arrive at the house to fix up for the shower, Sabrina notices she could sneak off and make a quick run while no one was paying her any attention. She jumps in Daddy T's truck and she end up at the cement warehouse. Sabrina makes her purchase, and she was back at the house before her kids could miss her. The tables and chairs start to arrive, the beginning process of the decorations was coming along great. Maxine drove by in a uber and seen the house being decorated so she knew something big was about to take place. The uber driver dropped her off at her friend Kat's house. Her and Kat had been friends for a while Kat was the one who introduce her to Ali. Maxine arrives at the house and was in motion to ring the bell, but the door swung open instead, Kat had seen her on the camera walking up. "OMG how the hell are you friend," Kat greeted her with a warm and long embraced hug. "I had nowhere else to go I just need to clear my head; I'm still shaking and upset behind my daughter's death". Of course, you are more than welcome here don't feel like a burden". Maxine goes into details about her, and Ali split up and she reiterated about shondrella death. Maxine laid it on thick about how Donald's family beat her up and she was hospitalized for days with injuries. "OMG your face looks horrible, whoever did this should be in jail". Kat cooked her some homemade soup and gave her some fresh clothes to put on, Kat also put antibiotic ointment on her bruised face. They continued to talk, and Maxine was finally feeling relaxed. Maxine had Kat wheeled in Kat was feeling so sorry for her. Kat has never seen the weird side of Maxine she only knows the good church going cannot do no wrong Maxine. Maxine asks Kat for a pen and paper she stated she needed to write a letter. "No problem let me get it out of my office". Kat returned with the items and Maxine begins to write a letter, Kat had a look of confusion on her face. Maxine had written a two-page letter. She gave Kat instructions that if she does not hear from her in a week to go to the police with this letter. "What the hell or you involved in Maxine" "Nothing at all I don't trust the family that beat me up, I feel they may come after me and this time even kill me". Well, why won't you get a restraining order or some type of court protection, you can't keep running around scared that people are after you, that makes no sense". "Just trust me on this one and honor my wish please". Kat tried to get Maxine to stay with her, she offered her free room board and promised to help her get back on her feet. Maxine declined but told her if she ever needed her, she would return. Kat continue to beg her, Kat was feeling like Maxine was not well she could not put her finger on it, but she had a weary feeling about Maxine's behavior. When Maxine left Kat called Ralph, but Monica had changed Ralph's number, so she had no luck. Maxine had nothing but revenge on her mind for her daughter and herself. During her walk to the store to purchase a phone, she had a run in with some dogs they chased her for a few seconds until the owner came out to retrieve them. A light bulb went off in her head and the inner crazy in her begins to smile. She speeds walks to the junk yard to find old man Louie. Old man Louie owned a junk yard, and he had a farm of dogs, people would find stray dogs and bring them to him, people would donate dogs as well. Louie was the dog catcher for all surrounding areas. Louie also had an area where he breaded dogs. Louie had dogs from mutts to pits to German Shepherds, Bulldogs, Rottweiler, Great Danes, poodles, Golden Retriever, and Boxers. Louie was in the middle of feeding some of the dogs when Maxine walks up. "Hello Ma'am, how can I help you". "Hello Mr. Louie, My name is Maxine Blackwell I'm married to Ali Blackwell, we came her a few times in the past for some car parts". "My reason for visiting you today is I have a proposition for you". "That sounds good if money is involved"." Yes indeed". "Well tell your story". "I need twenty of your biggest dogs, and I need to rent one of your moving trucks to place them inside, I have 800 dollars and the thing is you will get the dogs right back after I'm done". "I will call you and give you the area to pick them up". "Sounds good to me, just hand over the cash and I will load them up for you". "Can you drive a stick Shift Ma'am"? "Yes, sir I can handle that". Old man Louie goes and loads up the dogs, hands Maxine the keys and his business card, and explained that he was available 24 hours. He also explained that the dogs are not use to a lot of noise, so if they hear too much noise, they will go hay wire. Vernetta had out done herself the decorations were superb she had a co-worker of hers carve an ice sculpture of a baby, she placed a blue and pink scarf around the neck. There was blue and pink cupcakes and a fully loaded candy buffet table. It was sectioned off by sides, the blue side and the pink side. The chairs covers were pink and blue. The scenery was so nice the family could not get themselves dressed from being caught up in the view and luxury of the shower set up. Donald and Courtney would be arriving from the airport in 1 hour. Daddy T had the grill smoking the whole neighborhood was smelling good. Steak, pork chops, lobster tails, chicken, hotdogs, and burgers were just few of the food spread. Some of the guest had start arriving. The sisters were hosting and appointing people to sit on either the pink or blue side. The DJ had the music playing and Vernetta and Sabrina had bust out doing the electric slide, and the guest joined in. The yard was filled with laughter and excitement. BG, Big C, Karizma, Cotton and Tuesday were hanging out front smoking loud away from the older folks. A white truck pulls up out front. No one questioned it because they all assumed it was a delivery for the shower. Maxine jumps out of the truck she was parked with the passenger side facing the crowd so when she got out, she could not be spotted. Maxine beats on the side of the truck to get the dogs fired up. Once she heard all the dogs barking, she pulls the lever on the truck up, the dogs got a whiff of the food and they all barged out the truck and runs towards the house. Maxine gets back in the truck and pulls off expeditiously. Big C along with the rest of the crew hears and spots these dogs coming their way. Cotton and Tuesday starts to scream Karizma and Big C starts to shoot they only hit two of the dogs the others made it to the back yard. All hell broke loose, they were running wild. Everybody screamed bloody murder the dogs attack all the décor they demolished the cake and ate the food from the grill. Daddy T had to stop Big C and Karizma from firing their guns again it was too many people around. Everybody had made it to the inside of the house while the dogs continue to destroy everything. BG starts to spray the dogs with the hose pipe, while Daddy T was spraying the fire extinguisher. The dogs finally drifted away, running away from the house like a pack of wolves. No one was hurt or bitten, but the family feelings were hurt. Vernetta was so crushed she wanted to antifreeze them dogs. Sabrina knew exactly who did this and she was out for blood at that moment she had a panic attack and kept repeating "that bitch got to go" Donald and Courtney exit the car and walk through the yard and could not believe their eyes, they spotted two dead dogs and a yard full of mess. "Cuz what happened man". Donald asks BG. Sabrina came out and told Courtney to go in the house and relax, she then pulls Donald to the side and gives him the run down on everything with Maxine. "You got to be kidding me" Donald shouted. "I wish I were, but that bitch is mine I want her head on a platter", this time she will not live to tell this story". Their main goal at this moment was to keep Courtney calm. Donald and Sabrina agreed to tell her about the dogs but not about Maxine, they were protecting her from stress and keeping the baby healthy. Sabrina was not letting this put a damper on her grandchild's gender reveal she had outback steak house cater them some food, Beauty and Bonnie went to Publix to get more cupcakes and the shower continued. As long as Courtney was smiling Sabrina and Donald was at ease. After dinner and much conversation, it was time for the big reveal. Courtney stood up and gave a thank you speech to everyone then she passed Beauty the envelope. "Well damn we know who the favorite sister is", Caz said out loud Big C and Z.Z. co-signed. Beauty got straight to the business after opening the envelope, "on the count of three, scream loud as you can your gender preference". 1,2,3, all you heard was BOY and one faint girl which was yelled by Courtney. Sabrina yells at Beauty to stop playing around and get on with it. "Ok Ma chill out be patient". Sabrina then jumps up to grab the envelope from Beauty, but before she could Beauty screams "IT'S A GIRL". Courtney says, "yes I knew it, I got me a little Courtney growing inside of me". Everyone starts to clap giving congratulations to her and Donald, Donald reaches over and hugs Courtney. Just then Beauty says "you all have been punked, IT'S A BOY" she turns over the paper that read BOY in big bold letters, the Hawaiian Doctor had the paper decorated with pictures of the ultrasound in blue ink. You would have thought you were at a WWE wrestling match how loud they were screaming and acting a fool. Donald teared up, he kissed Courtney with so much force leaving her lips wet. Courtney embraced him and replied, "bae I'm fine with that I just want a healthy baby". Alvin starts to do a silly dance and sings out, "I got a nephew, I got a nephew". "I won't be offended if y'all name my nephew after me". "If anything, his name will be Donald Tramone Murphy Jr. "Nope you both wrong said Courtney his name is Champion Danarious Murphy". "As long as he a Murphy I'm game said Alvin" he and Donald dap hands and shared a laugh and hug. Dacember thought it would be the perfect time to tell Alvin about her little secret. Her and Alvin had been creeping around for almost a year and no one had a clue. She was pregnant herself; she was scared shitless to tell her sisters and Sabrina. So, she pulled Alvin out back and spilled the news to him, his mouth flew wide open, and he stood there in total shock. "So, what we going to do," said Alvin. "I'm not having no abortion if that's what you are thinking", "HELL NO, that's not what I was implying, I'm just a bit nervous I'm scared of your mom". "I am only two months so we will let Courtney shine with our nephew then we both drop the bomb on everyone together".

Chapter 24

PLAY WIT IT

DONALD SENT COURTNEY AND Beauty shopping for the baby, while he and Sabrina met up at his art gallery. Sabrina pulls up at the gallery. When she exited her car, she spots Monica going into Ralph's law firm. Sabrina makes her way across the street to speak with Monica. "Good morning Miss lady can we chop it up for a few minutes". "Sure" Monica said with a smile, "Don't smile yet the bitch still breathing". "Mercy" Monica responded. "I know your husband still have his men keeping a watch on Maxine, I need to know the bitch location ASAP". Sabrina went into details explaining the dog episode. Monica said in disgust "I don't put nothing past that sicko". The two bashed Maxine's name for the rest of their conversation. Before Sabrina walked back across the street, she handed Monica a card with her number. When Sabrina made her way to the gallery, she begins talking asking for any suggestions on what to do about Maxine. "I know one damn thing I will not get an ounce of sleep until that bitch is cold," said Donald. Alvin chimed in "it seems like the situation is not going to stop, the shit must be hereditary her parents must be cousins or related somehow". Everybody buss out laughing, but Sabrina was not in a laughing mood. "Let's stop having a Kumbaya moment and get out and find this bitch". "I have an informant working on her location right now" Sabrina said. Big C responded, "I got a rental jeep, so we gone ride till the wheels fall off, we fucking her up on site". "Y'all all know Courtney and Beauty is not to know shit, keep them busy while we handle business" Sabrina announced before they all exit the gallery. Two days had passed by and no sign of Maxine anywhere. It was hard for everyone to proceed with everyday life because Maxine was so unpredictable it was like walking on eggshells. Sabrina received a text from Monica, that read; Maxine is staying with a friend name Kat her Government is Katrina Smith, the address is 1000 Jenkins street in Pickens. Kat leaves the house every day for work at 10am, Maxine leaves the house around noon time to walk Kat's dog. Sabrina took a ride to her secret hide out to make sure she had all her ducks in a row. Sabrina had this day all planned out and was certain to cover her tracks.

Taking a page out of crazy bitch handbook, Sabrina bribed a delivery guy to use his van to spy on Maxine. The plan was to catch her out walking the dog and snatch her ass up. She knew Maxine would be on alert, so she had to blend in with the scenery. After 2 hours of casually watching the house Sabrina notices a beaten and bruised Maxine limp from the house with a dog beside her. It took everything in her not to laugh out loud at the damage she had caused. Sabrina continued the delivery route just scoping out the neighborhood and paying attention to the route that Maxine took when walking the dog. When the deliveries were done, she had the driver take her to her car. She called Big C and Daddy T when she got in, "ok mission complete". She proceeded to tell them about the neighborhood layout and the route that Maxine took. She could not wait to describe how fucked up her injuries were, Still. After laughing for a while about her being a Ronda Rousey contender they hung up. Tomorrow was go time, Caz, Big C, Z.Z. and BG would all take separate cars and drive thru the neighborhood while Maxine was out walking the dog, when she least expects it "BAM", gotcho ass bitch. Since Donald wanted her head on a fucking platter Sabrina was determined to give it to him. The next day everything was going smoothly, the first two cars, Caz and BG, stared patrolling the neighborhood. Both confirming that Kat had left for the day and Maxine was spotted walking her to the door. BG went to back of the neighborhood where he could see the house but not be seen by anyone else, he then waited. He was the lookout. Caz went to the gas station just off the main road so she could see who was coming in and not be spotted by Maxine. About an hour later the other two cars pulled up, both SUVs. Daddy T and Z.Z. were in a Ford F150, while Donald and Sabrina were in a Tahoe. When BG gave to word that Maxine was out walking, they entered the neighborhood. One from each entrance.

Whoever gets to her first does the job, we cannot let her get away", Sabrina said. Everyone was on the phone but quiet, they were anxious to get this shit over with. Maxine must have felt something was up because she took a different walking route. Hey BG go head and call in the backup plan I'm not taking no Ls today", Donald instructed. Ten minutes later they all had parked and were watching everything unfold. Karizma was dressed in a cute adidas running short set with a matching hat over a blonde wig that was braided to the side. She looked like she belonged on the street and was out for a daily jog. Maxine stopped her when she ran past, "Ma'am I think I am being followed by my crazy ass abusive ex", she explained waving her hand over her injuries like it was obvious. "Can you please help me?" Karizma obliged introducing herself as Morgan and telling her she could come to her house and call for help. Maxine was thinking she would jump Morgan and take her car so she could get the hell away from here. She felt like a sitting duck. They arrived at a house and Karizma surprisingly used a key to get in. Big C just smiled, "My bitch is thorough as fuck". Everyone exited their cars and made their way to the house. When they walked in, two of Deuces guys had already hog-tied Maxine and were ready to put her exactly where Sabrina instructed them to. "How the hell you get access to a house so fast Big C questioned? "Bitch I own it. Surly you did not think I was out here living hood rich without actually getting rich", said karizma. "This just one of my properties and clearly it came in handy". "Boss shit 101, you already know when you sneeze, I'm gone bless you". The men loaded and gagged Maxine into the trunk of a car and went to the secret location. Donald and all the sister followed by Sabrina and Daddy T were in route to the secret location as well. "Remind me not to fuck with y'all sisters", Donald said during the drive. "Why you say that brother? Caz responded. Y'all put in work like niggas and be ready to ride from the gate". "So, I see life if full of excitement and loyalty in my new family". They had arrived at the old Winn-Dixie warehouse in Spring Mountain. They used that spot for a gun range, it had been closed for over twenty years. Big C and her crew, and Daddy T were regulars there they often made a field trip out of shooting guns. Sabrina had everything pretty much in order she just had to mix the cement. Sabrina was giving out orders and making shit quick as possible. She had the men lay Maxine down in a wooden box, the box could have pass for a coffin. She then barked at Daddy T to pour the cement on top of her. Daddy T with the help of Donald poured the cement over her entire body until she was fully covered. Sabrina then pulls out a battery-operated floor heater to dry the cement. Ounce it was halfway dry she gave a signal to pour another batch on top of the semi dry coat. Everyone knew she was going to do Maxine dirty, but they had no idea it would be this entertaining. Maxine could not move one bit; all she could do was open her eyes wide as saucers when she seen the cement being poured. This was one time they all were together and there was total silence. "Y'all mutha fuckas get you panties out your ass, you knew it was not about to be no baptism in here". "Bull-shit this was definitely a baptism just wasn't with water BG chimed in. "Let this batch dry completely, then you guys place it in the back of the warehouse along the wall with all the other bricks". "Throw some dirt and rust on top, make it blend in with the other junk". "We all guilty by association, we are going to continue on and not even think or mutter a word or even dream about this shit". The sister start doing a hand clap game like Pattie cake, they break out doing the old school dance the prep. They then put the cherry on top by singing Goodie Mob, "WHO'S THAT FUCKING WITH MY SISTER POW NOBODY NOW". Donald shook his head and buss out laughing. Donald was happy the shit was finally over, but he was serious about not wanting no smoke with them sisters. He damn sure was going to stay clear of Sabrina. He wondered what Courtney inner crazy side was like because the fruit don't fall far from the tree he thought to himself. After tying up the loose ends at the warehouse they all went to party at club Blu.

Chapter 25

THE SWITCH

LUCY CONTACTS KARIZMA ABOUT the situation she needed handled. It was getting hectic hiding Trix, people were starting to be noisy. Trix had been living in the motel room shower for months, she could not risk getting caught that would be her whole life gone. The motel was so run down you could see through the worn-out curtains. There was always a crowd on the same row so that's why Trix played it safe, and she never left the shower. She had made the space her own placing blankets and pillows in the shower, having candles burning on the counter. The aroma kept her company and relaxed, she still was disgusted by her living arrangements. Trix had to suck it up because nobody told her to become a bank robber. Trix did the bank robberies all for a 2021 range rover, she got greedy with the money stuffing the bags with much speed she stopped a mir of a second before getting caught both times. No one knew about the second bank robbery until days later after it surfaced the news. Trix was lucky because none of her money had dye pack, she got away Scott free with six million dollars between both runs. Karizma put some heat on the Doctor Duo telling them they will be rewarded with another blazing trick from Deuces fine collection of thots. Karizma threw in some bait to see if they could pull some string and make shit happen this week. Just so happen they were both scheduled to do the overnight shift Saturday, no other doctors would be on duty that night. The surgery room will already be sanitized and ready to go. Trix will just have to recover in one of Karizma's spots, she cannot go back to that filthy hotel and risk getting infection. Racqi sent Karizma a text giving her the time and location and other details of how to maneuver when they drop Trix off. He also needs a picture of what she wanted to look like. Karizma pass the news on to Lucy when Lucy text her the picture it was a picture of the rapper Mulatto, Karizma giggled to herself then forwarded the picture to Racqi. Just a few more days said Lucy to Trix. Trix wanted Lucy to stay cooped up in the room with her but she had to run the motel she was trying to keep shit normal as possible. Karizma wanted to see if Slick Rick was still on the straight and narrow. She had some deep shit she needed him to handle for her, but he had to be straight. Karizma pulls up on Slick Rick shooting dice in the hole, the hole was the hood shit gets down and dirty in the hole, Kool Moe Dee Wild Wild West song describes it best. "What up sis" Slick Rick said with much excitement. "I'm licking these niggas taking their stimulus check ". "What you got going on, you need me". "Yes, I come to politic with you, but take your time I got next". Karizma observed Rick he still had the pinky ring and the grill; his clothes were fresh and upgraded from the sweatsuits she left him with. So, if he could pass her last test, he was going to be her partner. Karizma and Big C needed some manpower. After they wrapped the dice game, they went to the crab bar to chop it up and fuck up some crab legs. "I need you to deliver this package for me to a nigga staying the Quake Shack", no words need to be exchanged just a simple drop off". "You know I got that sis". Before they left Karizma filled Rick in on some money moves she was about to put into play. "Sis I'm all in I never knew the meaning of money I smoked crack for over ten years", I'm obsessed with it now". "I can buy nice things take my lady friend places and do stuff for her; I was a fucking idiot for smoking that shit". Karizma looked sad but she was happy at the same time. Karizma gave slick rick a box filled with six ounces of hard, one of the ounces was cut up easy access for him to grab if he wanted to. Several straight shooters were in the box as well, to boost up the temptation. When Slick Rick got in his girlfriend's car, he tossed the box on the passenger side floor. The box opened and the components fall out, he picks them up and place them back in the box he did not even consider the option of taking nothing. He passes the set up with flying colors. Karizma updated Deuce on her plan of putting Slick Rick down on the big boy roster and permanently take him off the bench. Slick Rick was already doing executive work at a crack head level. Giving Rick a tittle will boost his moral and keep him on the straight and narrow. The weekend has arrived, it was Saturday morning time for Trix to head to the Hospital for her plastic surgery. Karizma and Lucy had Trix dressed in all black with a hooded pulled over her head. Trix made it to the van without being spotted, the surgery was not until 10am but leaving at 6am gave them a head start with be discreet. Once they arrived at the hospital, they followed the strict instructions from Dr. Racqi. A young intern who introduced himself as Dr. Racqi's son was there at patient pick up with a wheelchair to take Trix to her assigned floor for surgery. He gave Karizma and Lucy the time for pick-up which was 5pm. Karizma said to Lucy, "I know you two need a spot to chill while Trix recover". "I'm cool with lending out one of my spots but it's a ticket price on it". "No doubt just name the price and its yours. We may need to pay up for a year that will give us time to get our shit together". "As always money talk fam". They passed time and went back to the motel and instructed one of the house cleaners to get Trix old room back in order. Karizma was passing out product and taking orders from all the regulars not long after she was done, Karizma left to go get a quickie in from her boy toy Surge. Time had managed to slip away from Karizma she had dozed off after bussin some powerful orgasms. Lucy was blowing her up it was now 5:30pm, Karizma answered the last call "Ok Luc I'm on my way, my bad fam". Lucy was standing outside of the motel when Karizma pulled up, they were at the Hospital in 10 minutes. Pulling up at the pick-up area, this time Dr. Racqi was there with medication and leaflets with all the necessary after surgery information. Trix was loaded in the van still highly medicated it was fresh covers laid in the back ready for her to lay on, until they reached their new living location. They went back to the hotel to finish talking business and to get Trix prepared for the move. Karizma had them set up in a nice 3-bedroom 2bathroom ranch style home that sat on 3 acres of land out in Laurens County. No neighbors within walking distance and you could see any visitors coming before they arrived. It was the perfect hide out. She also hooked them up with a cover story and some clean cash, seeing as how all their money was from the bank robbery and could be traced. Karizma charged them a quarter million for her hospitality, and the leg work she put in to keep them comfortable. She will provide Trix a South Carolina Driver's license, birth certificate, and a social security card with her new identity.

Lucy was big on loyalty and knew that Karizma was a down ass chic and boss lady, so she showed her gratitude by giving Karizma a cool million. Lucy knew that if Trix would have been caught she would have gone down too for accessary. Karizma was their only go to person, and she never left them hanging. After getting them settled in and having groceries delivered, Karizma left and headed to the 'wash house'. She had to start cleaning her money, before anyone figured out, she was carrying that amount of currency around. Knowing that pussy was always one of the top money makers. Karizma opened a lounge called "The Gentlemen's Club". Shit was going to pop off strong because the numbers that she and Deuce cleared weekly from just a hand full of girls, kept them eating. When Trix recovery is complete her and Lucy will take lead and keep the Gentlemen's club stacking paper. Trix changed her name to Summer Floyd, she was no longer Tracy Fleming known as Trix. Summer was anxious to see her new look, but Lucy kept her patient and kept her mind clear of it. The two worked out and became fitness buffs, Summer worked out so much in that tiny bathroom at the motel, she grew accustomed to working out. Being quarantined for her recovery will not be so bad after spending months in that motel. Summer had upgraded to ranch from a sleazy motel she went from ashy to classy feeling human again. After their morning workout it was time for the bandages to come off. Lucy sanitized her hands and began to unwrap her face, after the bandages were off lucy gives Summer a mirror and she smiles instantly. She was beautiful as could be looking identical to the picture she submitted to the Doctor. Her confidence was at an all-time high, she already had long curly hair, with beautiful eye lashes and creamy caramel skin. Her look before the surgery did not fit the crime. Lucy gives her a hug then whisper in her ear, "NO MORE BANK ROBBERIES PLEASE"!

Chapter 26

THE SET UP

KAT HAD BEEN PULLING up at the police station with Maxine's written letter all week, she could not force herself to go inside, it had been two weeks and no sign of Maxine. The way Maxine disappeared from her home raises a red flag. Kat build up enough courage to go inside of the police station and she filed a missing report. She filled out tons of paperwork and was asked several questions. She contemplated about giving the officer the letter. As she was getting ready to walk out the office door the officer asked was there anything else, she could add to help the case. Kat then turned around and said, "I have this letter and I believe it has something to do with her disappearance". The officer read the letter then he called in a few more officers to read it as well. Officer Bonnifier asked Kat, "exactly what did Maxine tell you when she gave you this letter. "She stated that she was beaten up by this lady Sabrina Wilks and her family, and they were out to get her". She also believed they forced her daughter to kill herself months ago". "She made me promise that if I do not hear from hear in one week to take this letter to the police, but it's been two weeks I was certain she would return, and it would not come to this". "Thank you, Ms. Smith for your patience and your information". My partner Jennie Collins and I will start this investigation early in the morning, here is my card feel free to call me and if you hear anything please let us know". Kat rode home thinking about Maxine. Her mind was wondering where the fuck could she be, Kat also was thinking about Maxine's unusual behavior and wonder if that had anything to do with her vanishing in broad daylight like she did. Officer Bonnifier was at the office at 6am. Bonnifier was a hard ass detective who took his job way too serious. Jennie was not due at the office until 8am, Bonnifier had all the details given by Kat and the letter on a power point. He also had her medical records pulled from the hospital and that clarified her getting beat up. He had the pictures of her injuries in maximized to get a better look of her bruising. When Officer Jennie walks in, he was pulling records on Sabrina, which came back squeaky clean. She seemed like Mother Teresa adopting 3 girls raising them with her own 4 in a three-bedroom house, making 7.50 an hour working at a dry cleaner. Sending two of her daughters off to college, volunteering at the group home hosting food and clothes drives. She had been dating Terrence Hill for well over ten years, Bonnifier could not even fine a traffic violation on Sabrina. He starts to think did Maxine list the right person. Officer Jennie did point out a part in the letter that stated, "don't let her background fool you she is the devil and she's out to kill me". The detectives discussed the case all the way up until lunch time. They decided after lunch they would visit the hospital where Maxine resided during her injury. The detectives arrive at the hospital and take the elevator to the trauma floor. Bonnifier stops at the desk and ask for the head nurse, while Jennie walk around being observant. The nice young nurse said it would be a few minutes she is finishing up giving a patient a bath. Bonnifier nodded his head. Sitting in the waiting area where he met back up with Jennie they were about to walk to the vending machine, until a nurse walks up and extends her hand. "Hello, I'm nurse Beth McDaniel, are you the Foster family". "No ma'am we are detectives I am Thomas Bonnifier and this is my partner Jennie Collins". "DECTECTIVES, sir I assure you that Mr. Foster was going to die rather we did the surgery or not". "We know nothing about Mr. Foster, we're her to ask you about Maxine Hicks-Blackwell". OK you two can step inside the family room while I grab her chart, we kept on her". When Beth returned, she had the chart and a bag. "Maxine was treated here for 9 days she left in the middle of the night and never returned back". "She had sustained several facial injuries and a temporary wired jaw". "Did she have any visitors while she was here" Jennie asked. "No ma'am her brother was called, but his wife gave clear instructions that he was not to be bothered by anyone concerning his sister". "How was her behavior when she was here"? Jennie asked again. "She was very weird she often talked to herself about her deceased daughter, and she did lots of writing". "Here is the journal she left behind along with a watch and head scarf". Bonnifier thanked the nurse for her time and he and Jennie exited the hospital. Jennie looked over the journal while Bonnifier drove back to the station. "Maxine has over twenty paragraphs that says Sabrina is out to get her, she is naming Sabrina kids she also mentioning the name Donald Murphy". Jennie continued telling the stories Maxine had wrote down in her journal. The journal was enough for a judge to issue a warrant for Sabrina Wilks arrest. Waiting on the judge's decision to determine if they have probable cause to arrest Sabrina. After two hours of waiting, they get the green light to proceed. Sabrina and Daddy T were chilling at the crib drinking some cock tails, suddenly a loud hard knock attacks the door. Daddy T automatically goes in defense mode and grabs his piece. Sabrina swings open the door with an attitude from the hard knock. The police had her house surrounded, "Sabina Wilks", "yes I am Sabrina". "Ma'am place your hands behind your back you are under arrest for the disappearance of Maxine Hicks-Blackwell". "This has to be a prank I know damn well you're not arresting me about that retarded ass psycho bitch". Daddy T steps out and says, "this must be some kind of mistake, how the fuck is my fiancé responsible for someone's disappearance"? Bonnifier explained the evidence as he placed the cuffs on Sabrina. Jennie walks Sabrina to the squad car and gently helped her inside. "Y'all mutha fuckas got the game twisted". "I don't know what kind of salt that deranged lunatic is shaking on you dumb bum ass cops, but y'all got the wrong bitch". "Daddy T I'm good, these pigs don't scare me"! Sabrina yelled through the window". "Ma'am can you tell me what the fuck this is about, I'm not going to believe I'm being arrested for the disappearance of the most craziest, looniest, sickest female of all times". Jennie responded, "calm down Ms. Wilks there is no need to call Ms. Hicks names she is missing and could be in danger". Sabrina begins verbally attacking Jennie the whole ride to the station. "Fuck you and Ms. Hicks, I hope you get a cottage cheese yeast infection, and your ass hole explodes with the coronavirus. Walking into the station Jennie has Sabrina by the arm guiding her in the interrogation room, Sabrina set at the table and screamed for her cuffs to come off, she repeated I am not a fucking criminal. "Bonnifier walks in with his clip board, he says to Sabrina. "If you agree to talk calmy and reframe from using profanity,

I can remove the cuffs". Sabrina smacks her lips the let out a deep breath and shook her head yes. Bonnifier took off the cuffs, he then offered her a bottled water. "I'm going to give you time to plead your case but let me speak first". Bonnifier explained to Sabrina. "We have substantial evidence that you may be involved in the disappearance of Maxine Hick". "Maxine left multiple clues and hints that if she comes up missing that you and your family are responsible", we know about the fight and Maxine suffered some serious injuries you banged her up really bad". "Now you can speak". "I know how this shit may look but Maxine and her daughter has been fucking with my family for months". Maxine continues to blame my family for her daughter's death, her daughter took her own life and it's a proven fact that Shondrella was just as nutty as Maxine". "She is clearly setting me up because of that ass beating I gave her". "She deserved every blow, if I was a few years younger, I would have caved her damn chest in". "Maxine stalked my daughter and my son-in-law, she broke in my daughter's home, and that's not the half of it". "I have the slut on video, wiping her ass with the sandwich meat and taking a shit in a pan of spaghetti out of my daughter's fridge". "Where was the police when she kidnapped the Amazon driver and made him help her plot against my family". "So, it's your statement that you have nothing to do with her being missing". "Hell, no I want nothing to do with that bitch if she's gone then good for her, but y'all mutha fuckas need to let me go I was about to fuck the shit out of my man and deep throat his dick". Bonnifeir and Jennie stepped out of the room to discuss this matter with the chief and other detectives. They all scrambled their brain trying to get to the root of the situation. The lead detective made an announcement, "we have confirmed that Maxine did have a lot of mental issues and without a confession from Sabrina by law we can only hold her for 72 hours". "If no solid evidence appears, we must let her go".

Chapter 27

NOT AGAIN

DADDY T ALONG WITH the rest of the family were down at the police station trying to make since of the police arresting Sabrina. Big C was pacing back and forth along with Donald. Officer Jennie comes out and try to give the family comfort and get them to relax. "How the fuck can we relax when y'all pigs invade people's home and throw your mutha fuckan badge around falsely arresting people, y'all need to arrest them punk as cops who killed George Floyd". "You mut be Sabrina's daughter, you both have such a colorful vocabulary". "Yep, and I got a colorful foot that I will put in your colorful ass". "you need to calm down young lady, or I will lock your ass up for threatening a police officer is not what you want, the choice is yours". Jennie felt a rush come over her body when Big C was verbally aggressive with her, she stopped them thoughts immediately. Caz grabbed Big C and took her outside to get some fresh air. Jennie continued giving them the info about the 72 hour hold and explained that one person will be allowed to see her for 30 minutes. She then added, "if we have any more rude or disrespectful outburst you all will be asked to leave". "I apologize ma'am my family and I are appalled by these allegations". My fiancé is facing criminal charges behind an obsessed mental patient, that clearly got y'all on a wild goose chase". "The news will have a field day with this one, and that's not a threat that's a promise". Daddy T said while trying to hold his composure. Jennie was fed up with this family, so she was spiteful and made Daddy T wait for two hours before he could visit with Sabrina. Big C was outside on her phone explaining to BG about the fine ass detective just tried to handle him, Big C put emphasis on Jennie being sexy but shook it off by saying "fuck that she the enemy". When Daddy T finally made it to the interrogation room Sabrina had her head on the table, she was tired from all the police mumbo-jumbo. When she heard then door open, she raised up and smiled at Daddy T. The two did not discuss anything they just held each other's hand the entire thirty minutes; they knew they were being recorded and Sabrina and Daddy T started playing footsy, Sabrina then grabs Daddy T dick and licked her lips seductively, her and Daddy T continued to be touchy feely acting like school kids. Sabrina had an unbothered look on her face and kept smiling and winking at the camera, aggravating the fuck out of Jennie. Sabrina knew Daddy T and Donald were about to get her out of there. Donald had pulled up at Ralph law firm hoping he was there. Ralph was unavailable but his wife Monica was there finishing up some paperwork before closing. "May I assist you with anything", Monica asks. I hate that we keep meeting up under these strange and deranged circumstances". "My mother-in-law is being held for the disappearance of Maxine". He explained the whole letter and journal situation and the verbal allegations of the friend Kat. He continued spilling all that he knew. Monica assured him that Ralph would be contacting with him before the night ends. Monica damn near had an orgasm, she was finally clear of Maxine and Shondrella. Monica knew Sabrina had eliminated Maxine; she did not need no details, but she was about to get Ralph to clear Sabrina's name. Sabrina was moved to a holding cell she was free from other inmates because she was only being held at this point. Jennie asked Sabrina did she need anything before she left for the night. Sabrina responded, "naw you just go home and get some dick, give that raunchy pussy of yours a treat so you want be so uptight tomorrow". Sabrina blew Jennie a kiss; then rolled her eyes hard like woman do when they are disgusted with somebody. She grabbed the blanket to cover her head and proceeded to lay on her bunk. Jennie wanted a round with Sabrina, she was fed up with her mouth but instead she took the high road and walked off. Ralph came home to a nice home cooked meal. The table was set up nice wine was poured, and Monica had two joints rolled, which she was smoking on one. Ralph thought he had forgotten their anniversary for a minute. "What the hell got you feeling so loose tonight"? Ralph asks Monica. "I can't be nice to my husband who I love so much". "Yes, you can so I assume

I'm out of the doghouse, and things are back to normal with us". "Not quite yet". "Tell me what's on your mind Ralph asks while reaching for the joint". Monica goes into deep details about what was going on with Sabrina. She suggested what she felt like he should do. Ralph let her finish her plea and he begin to rub on her ass feeling a bit froggy from the weed, he was ready to jump his wife bones. "You must have forgot who I am and what I stand for out in these streets, I am no rookie and this damn sure not my first rodeo". I already knew about the situation, but I'm glad to get you loosened up on a nigga". "I knew this situation was going to become ugly; I hate that it came to this, but I did all I could". They just couldn't leave well enough alone". "I also would like to thank you for not leaving me during all my involvement and making you so frustrated so many times, you have been my rock through this whole mess with my family". "Ralph, you tried so hard, it is not your fault we must move forward and forget about this fuckery". Ralph and Monica were able to do something they have not done in months, and that is fuck. Ralph started out passionate being delicate making love to his wife, but Monica turned into a beast and her inner tiger came out. So, Ralph gave her what she was yearning for, he fucked an arch in her back all night. The next morning Ralph was moving kind of slow. Monica was up cooking breakfast she limped around the kitchen score from the dick down she received from Ralph. Ralph joined her in the kitchen" good morning wild lady" Ralph said as he kissed Monica on her cheek. Monica blushed feeling a bit embarrassed, she had not smoked weed in years and the weed Ralph keeps in his stash is grade A loud, and apparently it tuned her into a bedroom salvage. Ralph and Monica ate their breakfast, then got dress and they both headed out to the police station. Ralph calls Donald and Daddy T and told them to gather up the family and meet them at the station. Ralph walks in with his briefcase in one hand and holding his wife hand with the other. Ralph approach the desk and ask for Bonnifier and Collins with much curtesy. "I'm sorry sir there in a meeting right now, you're more than welcome to wait" the desk cop responded. "See that's why you are behind a desk I will not wait". "Get them out here now, the chief, the sheriff somebody of some authority needs to be having a conversation with me ASAP". Ralph must have done a Beyonce and ringed the alarm, 30 seconds flat all the big wigs were in attendance. Mr. Hicks what do we owe the pleasure", one of the detectives said that was familiar with Ralph. "I see you all are holding my client Sabrina Wilks in custody for the disappearance of my sister Maxine Hicks-Blackwell". "Yes, we are, she's on a 72 hour hold while we further investigate the evidence" Bonnifier said loudly. "I suggest you pipe that down white boy, that information I already know I'm a lawyer I didn't come down here to eat donuts and drink coffee with you dummies". "I have a recorded phone message from my sister that she is out of town with her Suga Daddy getting served all the way around, my sister may be off her rocker, but she likes to get her ass played with like the average woman". "Maxine has venom in her heart for this family, she blames them for the suicide of her daughter, which is my niece". "If you would have did your homework and not base your entire case on a damn letter that anybody could have wrote, maybe you guys would have known that". The detectives looked crushed; they all were speechless. "I need my client released immediately, I have the local news out front to back up my story, how a black community volunteer woman gets falsely accused of the disappearance of a mental patient". "You fellas and ma'am have a Tony the tiger great day". Ralph along with the family goes to wait in the lobby for Sabrina to be released. Daddy T was the first to dap Ralph and praise him for his bravery with the officers. "Damn I see why you the man you just served them crackers with no cheese, that's what's up I appreciate that". Donald co-signed the appreciation, do we owe you anything fam"? "You were awesome". "Let us just be friends that's all I'm asking said Ralph. Monica rubs Ralph on his but his wood starts to rise, he said "alright you already limping". Bonnifier had Jennie to go and get Sabrina ready for release. Jennie frowned up; she did not want to be bothered with her especially after Ralph just tore them all a new ass hole. When Jennie walks up to the holding cell Sabrina was in there doing sit ups like she was doing hard time. "OK ma'am you are ATW lets go". Sabrina said and you are a P.I.G". "Not today please, that's police term for release". "Why so soon y'all found Maxine". "Actually, your attorney knows his shit, and the fact of him being the brother of Maxine helps you out a lot". "Well hurry up and open this damn gate, I can go home and catch Days of our lives" and catch up on my dick sucking game". "Don't look at me like you're not sucking these officers dick around here, I smell the mixture of donuts and nut on your breath; the stains on your teeth tell it all". "All the Colgate in the world can't remove that". Jennie wanted to back hand Sabrina so bad, but she just sped up the process getting her gone, Jennie prayed she never see her again. Sabrina enters the lobby and the family clapped so loud; the officers looked back but would not dare say nothing. All her daughters run up and hug her. Sabrina said, "let's get the fuck out of here this place gives me the creeps". Daddy T held her hand as she walked over to Ralph, Ralph extended his hand and said" no caption needed". Sabrina shook his hand, then she gives Monica a hug, telling her we must do lunch". "Ralph instantly says" she will not be hanging out with you; "I can't bail both of you out". They all laughed as they exit the station.

Chapter 28

SHE'S GRIMMY

KARIZMA HAD THE GENTLEMAN'S club up and running. Summer and Lucy were handling business keeping things together from the money to the tricks. BG and Big C held the security down, it was running like a family-owned establishment. Lucy and BG had been crushing on each other giving one another the I wanna fuck look. Lucy could not even pour her drink at the bar for lusting at BG. Summer walks by and spots her mouth open and studied the look on her face, she made a mental note of it and quickly brushed it off. BG goes and joins Karizma and Big C in VIP. "What's up with your girl Lucy"? BG asks Karizma. "Why, what she do curse your ass out"? "Hell, no if she keeps winking at me and licking her lips, I'm going to fuck around and put some dick in her life". "Nigga Lucy sucking pussy she doesn't want no dick in her mouth", Big C said jokingly. "I thought that too but your girl ready to convert back and I'm gone be the lucky one to do it". "I am about to put some dick in her life, bumping cooties a'int cutting it, Lucy wants some meat sis BG said proudly while holding his dick print". As time went on BG and Lucy continued with this school kid crush, it was becoming obvious, their flirtatious ways had all the club staff talking. Summer confronted Lucy with the rumors. "You can't believe everything you hear Summer I'm just doing my job; "I don't pay him any attention". "Bull-shit Summer replied I see the way you look at the nigga you can barely work the from trying to be cute". "You have the bar so backed up with people trying to get drinks, I see the gap you spread in your legs when he around". "Girl, stop damn tripping you must be on something, that coke fucking with your mental". Lucy walks away and go out back to smoke the half of blunt she had in her purse. Big C and Karizma notices her look of frustration so they followed her. "What up Luc"? "Shit, Summer tearing my damn nerves up". "Bitch don't act like you don't know why she is tripping; we know all about you and BG" Big C ranted. "What the fuck you gone do hoe", Karizma said while doing a dance. "Is it that noticeable", Karizma and Big C both yells out "YES". "You can't have them both somebody going to end up hurt, you better put your big girl panties on and pick a side". Said Karizma. "Yes, girl no straddling the fence honey because shit gone get real" Big C added. Lucy and Summer's home was full of tension, it was so thick you could slice it with a knife. Lucy tried to make herself have sex with Summer but all she could think about was BG. Summer noticed her being standoffish, so she pulls out a dildo strap on" here bitch since it's dick you want ill fuck you, turn your ass over, bust it open for this plastic dick". Summer kept tormenting Lucy; they end up fist fighting tearing up the damn house. They both end up with bruises to the face. The next night at the club Karizma had a brief meeting with all the staff about some general club information. She notices that Lucy had this long red scratch down the side of her face, then she gets a glance at Summer and she had a few knots on her head. She thought to herself what the fuck these girls doing, and she really hoped they was not fucking up her property. Karizma had been hearing from Slick Rick that Summer was playing with her nose sniffing that booger sugar, her attitude and demeanor had changed tremendously. BG stepped his game up and asked Lucy can he take her out, Lucy happily excepted. Summer had a part time job at the gym, so she used that time to kick it with BG. They went to an ice cream parlor, they stared at each for the first ten minutes. Then BG spoke. "What's the deal between you and ole girl". "Basically, I helped her out of a situation, and we became close, one night after one too many drinks we both got promiscuous and curious, and that lead us into a situationship". "So is that permanent or just a temporary fix". "I'm not even into girls that was something I just got caught up in, we were vibing so well I just really needed a best friend, but things ended up going too far". "Seeing you made me realize I'm living a lie". "So, what you are saying I can shoot my shot". "If you like what you see you can". "Damn skippy", but first you need to end shit with your people I don't want to be in the middle of a love triangle ya feel me". BG and Lucy continued to talk, they realize they had a lot in common and they were in the same circle of people and that made them feel warmed up to each other. BG kissed lucy softly on her lips and they both went their separate ways. Lucy returns home and Summer was already there, Lucy had lost track of time being mesmerized by BG. "Where the hell you been", Summer said. "I had some business to handle for Karizma and don't be fucking yelling at me". "You a mutha fuckan lie you been with that nigga I can smell his cologne on your dumb ass". "So, if you knew why the fuck you ask". "We need to get up with Karizma and see what to do about the house because I'm moving out shit just not working out, all you wanna do is sniff powder and fuck its more to life than that". "Oh, so you get a little boy toy and now I'm not good enough for you, before the club opened you were sucking my pussy like a leach and taking dildos in the mouth until you choked". Summer went on for an hour cursing and packing her clothes at the same time. "Fuck you Lucy you better hope I calm down if not I'm fucking you and your fuck boy up". Summer slams the door and she left in her car speeding up the country dirt road. Lucy calls Karizma and give her heads up on what had just gone down with her and Summer. She decided to move out the house herself, she was tired of living so far away from everybody in the country, Lucy was a city girl, and she was tired of bending over backwards just to please Summer. Lucy asked Karizma if she could put her in a small crib close to the Quake Shack. Karizma agreed. Karizma decided to call Summer to see what the deal was about the house. Karizma went out her way to put her in that house so she felt it would be disrespectful to just leave. "Hello" "what up Summer, I just wanted to touch base on the situation with the house". "I see you and Lucy on a breakup or whatever y'all calling it". "Don't act like you are clueless on what the fuck going down, all y'all mutha fuckars know she is fucking that nigga BG". "Hold on pimpin slow your roll clearly you have no clue on who the fuck you are talking too". "Now I called just to get a visual on what's up with my property considering you rushed and moved out and apparently so did Lucy". "It doesn't matter if anybody is there or not, I paid you bitch, cash mutha fuckan money so just because I packed some clothes don't give you the right to be calling questioning my decision making". "I tell you what since you wanna bite the hand that feed you, this bitch is evicting your wanted ass", just in case you didn't know you're fired from my establishment". "You wanna be boss ass bitch, I don't give two fucks about that pussy ass job and you better be glad I gotta lay low because ill kick your black ass and show you who's boss". They went back and forth until Karizma finally hung up the phone. Karizma calls Big C and Lucy to meet up with them at the club. They all were sitting around the bar Karima starts to fill up s hot glasses with patron. "That's how we doing it tonight?" says Big C. "Man listen that bitch Summer Trix whoever the fuck the hoe is, she got the game twisted". Karizma gave them full details on there over the phone argument. "Lucy speaks up and says fuck that trick". "I'm certainly about to fuck BG now I don't know why I tried to convince myself I was gay, bitches worse than niggas". she has no one in her corner so it's a matter of time before she's calling to get her beg on". Karizma told Lucy she did not want her to get all mushy and have a change of heart, because Summer was not allowed nowhere near none of her properties. Karizma did not want Lucy involved with that chic anymore, the damage was done. Karizma calls Slick Rick and told him to pack up and go stay at the ranch Lucy was at, he told her he would do it tomorrow that he and his girlfriend was at Harrah's casino in Cherokee. "What's wrong sis I hear in your voice"? "That lil chic Lucy was fucking with trying to play me, I'll fill you in when you touch down, I'm not going to spoil you fun time". "Cool, you good thou"? "Yeah, Rick I'm good fam you know that; "you just concentrate on winning us that money Bro". Lucy moved in her new spot Karizma hooked her up once again. Lucy called BG over for dinner and a movie but instead it was drinks and a fuck session. The two chilled the rest of the night cuddling up getting deep in conversation, they felt like they been knowing each other for years. The next day they slept until the afternoon, they both were sluggish from the late-night drinks and tired from all the rough sex. They fucked like they had something to prove. BG hugs Lucy telling her he had to meet up with Big C at the club, Lucy did not want him to leave. "This is the beginning of a nice relationship no need to rush things" BG said with much swagger in his voice. When BG made it out front to his car, he could not believe his eyes, his car was on all fours and spray painted with orange smiley faces all over. Lucy came out to join him she was in a rage. "OMG, I know exactly who done this". Lucy runs in the house to get her phone and she dials Summer. Summer answers, "was the dick good tow service, how can I help you". "You are a real live psychopath, why the fuck would you do that". "Awww you mad because your boy toy has a few flat tires, he needs to thank me for adding some vibrant color to his whip, tell him don't be ungrateful". "Stay the fuck away from me bitch". BG called for a tow and he took Lucy's car to proceed with his day. BG was mad as hell but held his composure because he did not want Lucy to think he fight woman, but low key he was going to fuck summer up when he finds her. The gossip had gotten around how Summer had flipped her wig, Karizma had people looking high and low for her. BG was on the prowl himself. A few people from the hole had told Karizma that Summer was buying white girl, Summer was playing with her nose snorting grams of coke a day. Later that night Slick Rick and his girlfriend Jazz headed out to Karizma's ranch he was a few days late, but they were packed and ready to stay. As he was driving down the long dirt road his mouth flew open, and Jazz says out loud "what the fuck". The ranch was on fire burning to the ground. There was no need to call the fire department by the time they got there the house would be a memory. This was indeed arson. Slick Rick calls Karizma, "what up Bro", sis you are sitting down". Rick let it rip about the ranch, Karizma screamed out "ARE YOU SERIOUS", she snatched her keys off the bar and went running out the door. Surge was sitting down at the bar with Karizma he knew something was wrong the way she jumped up, Karizma had been telling him about Summer so he was right on her hills, he hopped in the car and rode with her. When Karizma arrived, there was nothing she could do, she just wanted a visual of this disaster of her own. Seeing something go down in flames that you brought to life sucks Karizma played in her mind. She was now more determined than ever to catch this chic she had stacks on her head.

Chapter 29

THE BIG PAY BACK

ALVIN HAD REACHED OUT to Karizma to book a guy's night at the club since he did not get to give Donald a bachelor shindig, he thought a turn up with his boys was much needed. They planned to shut the club down it became the talk of the town, all the ballers were exchanging big faces for singles so that could make it rain. Courtney did not even protest, she gave Donald permission to get one lap dance with one stipulation, she had to be via face time while the dance took place. Donald was sending her and Beauty and Bonnie, and Courtney's best friend Bella to Las Vegas. Slick Rick was hired by Donald to be their security. Rick was taking his boo thang Jazz along; he thought she would fit right in with them. The club begins to swell in capacity, VIP was vibing; and turnt all the way up. The dancers were at their best twerking trying to get that bag. Sabrina followed Daddy T to the Club she did not want to mop the floor with one of them young girls, for mistaking Daddy T for a Suga Daddy. Caz, Z.Z., and Dacember were also in attendance they pretty much followed Big C wherever she went. Big C and BG were out front handling the security, getting high off that good in between time. The dancers had to be making it clap because the crowd's volume was on 20. Just as BG and Big C were about to go see what the hype was about, they hear a loud engine roaring through the parking lot. They both jog to the lot, there was a colossal size monster truck at least 20 feet off the ground, driving over the cars that were parked in the lot. They begin to scream over the roaring engine trying to get whoever to stop. After several minutes, and thirty smashed cars later; the truck stops while on top of another car. Summer leans her head out the window and gives BG the finger. "BG said that's that crazy ass bitch Summer". "Oh, hell naw Big C screams, go get help we about to get this bitch out this mutha fuckan truck somehow". BG returns with the rest of security and Karizma, Lucy, Daddy T, and Sabrina were all in tow. BG started throwing bricks at the truck, doing everything he could think of to get at Summer. "Bitch, get your crazy ass down, stop fucking up these people cars". Lucy yells at Summer. "You won't answer my calls you keep fucking this fat dusty clown ass nigga; "you left me when I needed you the most". "What the fuck your nut-nut ass proving by doing shit like this". "Just get down we can talk". "Bitch I'm not that much of a nut-nut, you think I'm coming down so y'all can beat my ass". Summer gives her the finger and drives over the rest of the cars that was on that row she then pulls out the parking lot and speeds up the highway. Big C was about to get in her car and chase after her, but Sabrina stopped her. "Chelsea I'm not about to let you get in no high-speed chase with her, and risk getting killed or hurt no ma'am not on my watch". "Y'all know her situation, stop letting that bitch control shit". "Snitch on that bitch like the rest of these police ass niggas do in Greenville, the ball in your court". "She may have a new face, but her fingerprints tell it all, she wanna play games teach her ass this chess not checkers". "Big C said, "check mate", Karizma co-signed by saying "put me in the game coach I came to play ball". The night started out fun, but Summer put a damper on everybody's mood to continue to party. Karizma just shut the club down and told all 47 people that received damage to their cars that her lawyer will be contacting them all; she explained that her club's insurance will take care of their vehicle. No one blew up about it they knew they would be compensated; most people knew her credentials. Karizma and Big C were at the police station at 9 am sharp. They ask the man at the desk for Jennie Collins, he instructed them to have a seat. "Man, I feel like a fucking snitch", said Karizma. "Shiid I never ate cheese on a mutha fuckar either but this bitch gotta go fam, she doing the most". Jennie walks to the waiting area with her morning coffee in hand. "Wow if it aint potty mouth number two". "Did you forget some names you wanted to call me and decided to do a special delivery". "Is it just you two or is potty mouth number one lingering around the premises"? "No ma'am I have some useful information for you and your fellow detectives". "Really". "Let's take this to my office". Once they entered the office, Jennie offered them a seat. "Please tell me what bring you ladies to talk with the police today". "I'm going to keep this short as possible, I'm feeling awkward as fuck, but here it is". "My partner and I have solid information on the bank robberies that took place months ago". Big C said as if she was a businesswoman. Karizma chimed in, "we know exactly who she is and where you can catch her". "Do tell who is this woman that has rubbed you two the wrong way"? "This kind of information just don't just fall from the sky and drop in our lap". "We're going to move around the details and go straight to the subject at hand, I just need one thing in return". Karizama says. "You still have my attention," said Jennie. "The place where you will most likely apprehend her is a high drug and prostitution area, I know you are familiar with the hole". "I'm only giving her up the other activities need to be ignored, you along with all the other detectives need to turn a blind eye to any other crimes that may be going on". We are violating the code by even working with you, but we will not be responsible on anybody else going down by us giving her up". Jennie agreed to the terms. Karizma and Big C filled her in on the surgery and gave her name and all other possible locations she may be. A week later Summer had paid some teen boys to spray paint Lucy house she had been keeping track of her every move she was outside of Lucy's window listening in on her and BG having sex. Summer later went to the hole to get her daily fix she had plans on stalking Lucy and BG some more. Soon as she exits the car and walk towards the big green dumpster, where cripple Ken was posted up selling grams of coke bags. The jump out squad jumped out the back of a cable van and rushed her to the ground Bonnifier placed the cuffs on her and said Tracy Fleming you're under arrest your party is over Trix". Karizma receives a call from one of the Blossoms little sister Molly she informs her on what just went down. Karizma calls Lucy and Big C and they all head to the hole hoping to catch her before they pull off with her. They pull up just in time, Summer was being placed from the van to a squad car." Great job Mr. officer we need to get people like this off the street, let us give these good officers a round of applause for their hard work". BG said as he laughed at Summer, he then grabs Lucy and kiss her while smacking her on her ass. Karizma and Big C was clapping and making loud whistle noises. Before the squad car pulled off, they all sang" NA NA NA NA, HEY HEY HEY, GOODBYE!! Big C walks over to Jennie and blew her a kiss then said great job boss". She then calls Donald and give him the tea on Summer, "I sure hope this is the last of these obsessed ass females, I think I may open up a therapy clinic for woman". "This has been a hell of a journey dealing with women and their mental mind challenges" Donald said out loud, being so serious. "Bitches need to start swallowing and stop bringing these unstable babies in the world" Big C said". BG said naw they need to just gargle and spit that shit down the toilet, swallowing they can spit that shit back up and recycle it. They all buss out laughing. The next day Big C receive a call from detective Jennie she wanted to say thanks for the big tip helping them catch Trix. "Please don't thank me cause I'm no snitch or do I work with you pigs, I just needed that bitch gone and that was the only way." "Understandable, but this call is also a social call". "Look lady I don't know what the fuck you got up your sleeve, but it will not work that was a once in a lifetime deal, Big C said getting frustrated with Jennie". "I want to take you out on a date I don't know why but you excite me, and I like how I feel around you, I been thinking of you and your swagger". "I might be the po-po but I'm human". "How you know if I even like woman, I can have a 12-inch dick nigga knocking the bottom out my pussy". "Negative, I am a detective remember I know all I need to know, so what's up"? Big C has never been the mute type, but she was silent for minutes all kind of thoughts were blasting through her head, she finally spoke, "Let's do it". Jennie overheard Big C at the detention center say that she did not like her, but she called her sexy, Big c had mumbled that under her breathe after she cursed Jennie out for arresting Sabrina. Big C blowing her a kiss is what really put her in her feelings.

Chapter 30

NOT TODAY

THE WILKS SISTERS AND Donald's mom Vernetta were planning the baby shower for baby Champion. The family was so excited. Donald and Courtney were just to the moon with joy of having their first baby. They were very ecstatic to celebrate and shower their baby with gifts with family and friends. It was now January and Courtney was due to deliver next month. Courtney was schedule for maternity leave at the end of the week. Donald and Alvin kept a close eye on Courtney and had her chauffeured around to her every stop. So much drama that has unfolded right before their eyes the two brothers refused to chance anything happening to Courtney and the baby. Sabrina and Monica hooked up for lunch they both were in a good mood, now that the problem was taken care of. They both sit down at the outside bistro, after placing their order they begin to talk. Sabrina says, "Girl I really want to thank you personally on how you put your husband down to campaign for team Sabrina". "Them punk ass pigs were going to trump them charges on me, just to meet a quota". "I'm only glad that the hoe decided to find a man and leave us the fuck alone, Monica said as she winked her eye at Sabrina. "They don't have any other sisters or auntie's I need to be worried about do they". "Hell no, it was just them two nut buckets". "Well, you keep twirling that pussy on Ralph and keep him copacetic, so he doesn't have no kind of family relapse". Monica laughed until her belly was hurting. Monica and Sabrina had started A new friendship they begin to hang out and do business together and never discussed Maxine ever again. Big C was going on a scavenger hunt for the remainder of Trix bank robbery money, she felt like there was no need to let it go to waste or let the police confiscate it. She plugged Karizma, Lucy and BG in on the plan at hand. Lucy shared a few spots that she knew Trix to out hang at. They went to all the locations and searched them high and low. They kept coming up empty handed, but the money had to be somewhere they just had to find it. Slick Rick calls Karizma and give her the news on a man name Jack, who was renting a room at the Quake Shake. Right before Trix was arrested she came and took his room and rented him another room on the far end. Jack liked his room, but he was forced out by Trix. Trix had paid the room up for two months. Jack got word that she was arrested he wanted his room back. Jack got plenty of action in that room and he could keep a visual on what was coming in and out. Nobody wanted to hang out on the back side, jack was losing his company because he relocated. Karizma told the girls she had to go to the motel to handle a matter, after giving them details about the situation. A light snapped on in Lucy's head, "hurry up Karizma I know where the money at" "WHAT", "just trust me get to the motel ASAP. As Karizma was hanging curves speeding, violating every traffic law ever written. Lucy gave them details on the secret wall that her and Trix used to hide shit when they were in the motel room 226. Lucy would bet her right arm that the money was there, it was the perfect hiding spot. Trix hide the money thinking nobody would ever find it or think to look for it there, when she got the room the new gay guy Andre was working the desk. Trix placed the money behind several walls of sheet rock. They pull up to the motel and Slick Rick was out front waiting on them. Lucy went to the office and made a key for room 226. They all jog to the room, Slick Rick asking, "what is going on"? Karizma told him to just keep an eye out and do not let nobody near the room. Lucy goes in and starts to rip out the wall, she pulls away at the debris, the chalking dust feels the air she is going salvage. After a few minutes Big C and Karizma starts to help. Ten lovely minutes later they find a Bath & Body Works bag with three in a half million dollars laid flat in the bag, the Benjamins were still fresh and crispy. Karizma, Big C and Lucy got a million dollars apiece, Slick Rick and BG were given the half a million to split. Karizma said there was no need to fix the wall because she was about to demo the entire motel and rebuild, she had a free million dollars and was about to make it do what it do. The others felt the same, Big C was about to purchase everything for her sister's shower and buy all the polo baby clothes that the mall has. Slick Rick had a Kool-Aid smile glued to his face, "DAMN sis that's what hit a lick look and smells like". "Let's go to club blu and turn the fuck up, first twenty rounds on me said Lucy". Slick Rick boarded up the room before they took off. They gathered all the other family and friends and hit the club deep. They had VIP lit, from popping bottles to making it rain wilding out throwing money. The crew partied like rock stars till the wee hours in the morning. The baby shower was taking place at Donald's art gallery the next day. Vernetta was not letting no dogs are even squirrels ruin this event. The cost of this baby shower was well over ten stacks. This family was all in and spared no cost for this day. Courtney was dressed in a baby blue maternity dress, Donald and the rest of the family and guests had baby blue t-shirts that said waiting on the Champion. Big C had so many gifts she had to order a truck to deliver them. When the driver pulled up in the white truck Vernetta spots the truck, she grabs her pistol out her purse and said, "oh hell no not today". The driver gets out the truck and he start to call Big C to alert her he had arrived. Just before he made his call Vernetta puts her pistol to his head and spoke, "hold your mutha fuckan hands up and back away from the truck right now". Vernetta's sounded notorious and serious. The driver starts to state his business but Vernetta did not give him a chance, she shot the driver twice in the leg. The driver grunted in pain, damn lady I'm no attacker I'm here for Big C". Everybody comes running when they heard the shots. Sabrina says first "what the fuck is going on now, Daddy T get my shit"? "MA" you alright said Donald"? "Did this mutha fuckar hurt you", "hell naw this man was about to do something crazy, so I put something hot in his ass". "I'm not letting nobody mess this baby shower up for my grandson". "Donald bends down to ask the driver what his purpose was for being there, he explained that he was hired by Big C. "Mama V, are you ok Big C asked" she was slightly tired from running from the back. Donald hit her with the 411. Big C cleaned up the miss-hap, and Donald and Alvin repeatedly apologized to the man who was a handy man named Bobby Timms. The brothers tried to correct their moms wrong, so they blessed the man with five stack a piece, charming him with hush money. Alvin basically had him shook up and dared him if he looked at his mom wrong it was going to be more bullets in his ass.

Alvin felt bad for Bobby, but he had to eat that one he was protecting Ma Dukes by any means necessary. Bobby was bent over in pain, he explained everything was all good, he had so much crack in his system he was still high from last week. "Big C offered to take him to the Emergency Center, Bobby stated, "I got warrants, and besides this ain't shit a screwdriver and some rubbing alcohol can't fix, hell for another ten stacks she can shoot me in my other leg". Vernetta walks back in the gallery to skirt her tables like she did not just shoot a man. Donald looks at Alvin and laugh and says that's defiantly your mom". Alvin responded, "between mama and your mother-in-law, we need to hire the damn secret service". After the baby shower was finished being set up, the festivities had begun. Courtney had a maternity photo shoot showing off her big baby bump. There was a cotton candy, frozen slushie, popcorn, and a full snack bar station. Courtney and Donald received over 200 gifts. Sabrina had all the men put fake pregnancy belts on and gave them a taste of how woman feel carrying a baby. A game was played with the men racing around the fire cones. This was a hilarious moment Daddy T, Donald, BG, and Alvin and a few more men were wobbling through the cones, they looked so tired and out of breath after 5 minutes. Several more games were played but none compared to this one. Ralph and Monica came in after the men took off the belts, they insisted on Ralph completing the exercise for the fun of it. "Hell, naw we just came to support the new parents to be I make babies not have them". Donald pass Ralph a joint to light up and hugged him across the neck and said, "I am going to let you slide fam because I may be needed a lawyer for my mom running around here shooting people". "Dammit boy, I really got to keep my wife away from the woman of this family". Sabrina says, "not a chance she's my honorary cousin, come on Monica let's get a drink a show these young folks how to twerk something". There are so many gifts, so Donald started a soul train line, showing off a gift while he dances down the line. The rest of the guest followed his lead, some of the guest did a model walk with the baby gift, they made it so much fun. Two hours of showing of the gifts the shower was complete, people were packing up plates and saying their goodbyes. Courtney wanted all her gifts home so her Beauty and Bonnie could decorate the baby room, but there was no way all the gifts could go in cars. Good thing Bobby had hung around out front. Bobby did just what he said, he took the bullets out of his leg and cleaned the wound with rubbing alcohol. Alvin was in disbelief of him not needing medical attention, he said out loud "crack is a hell of a drug". Alvin then had Bobby to help reload up his truck with all the gifts and do another drop off, this time he will be safe from his mom she was out the way.

Chapter 31

THE CHAMP IS HERE

EVERYTHING AND EVERYONE WERE doing great. Karizma being the kick ass businesswoman she is, started renovations on the Quake Shake, deciding to rename it sleep with a twist, and turning it into a extended stay motel. The rooms would all have well-stocked mini bars and snack baskets. Her guests would be able to enjoy an Olympic sized pool and casino and full bar, not to mention the wing spot along with strip club. All of this was to be on the premises. For the kids there was a Go-Kart fun park. Her ideas were making her big money already and she kept revamping everything to keep the money flowing in. Deuce made Blossom his bitch. She ended up loving his broken dick. She reasoned that one broken dick with money, that cashed out on her was way better that ten hard dicks, that had to be fucked and sucked for a buck. Blossom actually had feelings for Deuce she was just trying to fight it. Her beating all the other females out of the top spot by becoming wifey to Deuce makes her feel like she is that bitch. Slick Rick and Jazz tied the knot and just bought their first house together. Unfortunately, Trix got sentenced to 120 months. She had to do her time in Austin, Texas at the Federal women's prison. Daddy T finally convinced Sabrina to settle down with him and be his wife. Big C had found love, but her sneaky ass was keeping everyone in the dark about the specifics of her relationship for now. She knew firsthand how extra her family could be and did not want to subject her boo thang to all that just yet.

Donald and Courtney were still very much in love and awaiting the arrival of their bundle of joy. Donald was currently trying to plan a small Valentine's day dinner at the house for Courtney. He wanted to cheer her up because she had some constant back pain causing her to mope around the house. Donald had reached out to Bella, her best friend for help. Bella was also a physical therapist and could help ease some of the discomfort she was experiencing. Bella gave her a soft tissue massage and it helped for a little while and Courtney was able to get a good nap in. Donald finished up dinner and woke his wife. She did not really eat anything, just kind of pushed the lobster and steak around with her fork. "What's wrong my love?", Donald asked concerned. "I feel like I'm going to throw up. No offense to the food, it smells great but horrible at the same time. My mouth is watery, and my back is hurting again.", she said with the saddest face. "Just lay on the couch and get as comfortable as possible, I will put everything up and you can eat later", Donald began helping her up. "We can lay on the couch and watch Netflix. I will rub your back for you", he offered. She just nodded. Before they made it to the couch a gush of water ran down her leg followed by a sharp pain. "OWWW!", Courtney yelled out. "Bae, I think it's time". Those simple words sent Donald into full panic mode. "Ok. Ok. "Let me wash the dog and take out the trash", Its going to be ok", he said in confusion. "Nigga what the fuck are you talking about, get my damn bag and let's go". "The baby is coming", Courtney yelled in frustration.

Donald was so anxious, he was running around like a chicken with its head cut off, going everywhere and nowhere at the same time. He did not know what to do. He started to pack a bag for them, trying to remember everything what was needed, but Courtney had packed a bag weeks ago. While Courtney stood there in disbelief while Donald literally lost his mind, a hard contraction hit her. It sent her bending over the couch. Shit was getting real. She called for him, but he was pissing in the trash can. "Alvin, get over here now, it's time; the baby is coming", Courtney managed to call Alvin, who stayed two streets over. "On the way sis", was all he said. Since he was so close, he made it to the house in record time. "Alexa call Beauty", Courtney thought to call at least one of the sisters. By the time Beauty answered the phone Courtney had another contraction and all she could do was scream into the phone. Beauty understood exactly what was going on and she hung up, only to call all the other sisters and Sabrina. Having a spare key

Alvin let himself in, to find a mad house. Courtney was bracing herself on the back of the couch trying her best to breath while Donald was putting the bag full of piss in the freezer, the poor man could not put two and two to get four to save his life. Or in this case his wife's life. "What the actual fuck?", Alvin said mostly to himself. He immediately jumped in helping Courtney to the car so he could get her to the hospital. He managed to wrangle Donald before they went.

By the time Alvin got them to the hospital door, the call had gone through. The family and everyone were scrambling to get to the hospital. Sabrina managed to meet them at the hospital she was there in time to wheel Courtney into labor and delivery. "Alvin help your brother get his shit together", Sabrina barked. Only one person could go back there due to Covid-19, so she was going to stand in until Donald could get it together. "Bro, snap out of it", Alvin slapped his brother. "You finna be a daddy nigga. Tighten up". Donald was stuck. Dragging his brother just outside, "Here smoke this", handing him a half of a blunt full of pressure. While Donald calmed his nerves, Alvin called their mom letting her know what was going on. "I'm already on the way son, please look out for Donald, I know he is panicking", she said before hanging up. "You good now nigga", he asked Donald. "Yeah man, I don't know what is wrong with me". Patting his brother on the back the two walked back into the hospital. "Bro. What do I do. What if I freeze up?", Donald had real tears. Alvin hugged his little brother tight. "You got this bro and I got you. You will be simply fine. Now go be there for your wife and kid. They need you." Donald began to calm down and relax, thanks to the loud he just smoked. A nurse got him dressed for labor and delivery and he relieved Sabrina.

The doctor let Sabrina stay once Donald came in the room, she just had to stay out of the way. Courtney had a fit when her mom stepped away from her, so they had to do something to keep her calm. She had refused an epidural, Beauty convinced her that any drugs during delivery was going to cause mental complications. After dealing with Shondrella and Maxine, Courtney would not risk anything. "Courtney baby, you better take that damn shot and stop listening to your sister. You are in to much pain and your belly look like it's getting bigger." Sabrina said trying to convince Courtney to agree to the meds. She was not hearing it. Dr. Bailey, her OB-GYN, had taken the vitals and measurements to see where they were in the delivery process. "Courtney, I have figured out why you are in so much pain. Your baby is measuring 12 pounds dear". "12 pounds, damn girl. I told you to lay off those crab legs and baked potatoes", Sabrina joked, trying to keep her baby calm as possible. The nurse signaled for Donald. "Daddy, you can stand right here". He took his spot and immediately began coaching her to breathe and telling her how good she was doing. "Baby I love you and you are doing great", he said into her ear while holding her hand. After a few more hard contractions, and baby kicking violently, Courtney begged for the damn epidural. Donald was there for it all. Holding her hand through everything.

After the anesthesiologist left, and Courtney was settled, she began to doze off. At first Donald got scared but Dr. Bailey explained that she was not 10 centimeters. "Mr. Murphy your wife is doing fine. "The medication has made her sleepy", she is not ready to push just yet, she must dilate to 10 before the baby can come into the world". "So now it is a waiting game". With the lights low and soft music playing, Donald rubbed circles on Courtney's back while she rests. He talked to the baby, "Hey Champ. I need you to do what you are supposed to do. Mommy is trying her best, but I think she is tired. So, you gotta help me out man.". He saw the baby move at the sound of his voice. ", I just need you safe and healthy". About 2 hours later the doctor returned to check, "Its almost show time, we are 8 centimeters and growing.". The nurses came in and started setting up machines and getting everything ready for the big show. "Alright sweetie, I need you to sit all the way up and put your legs in the stirrups", the head nurse instructed. By the time they were ready for pushing it was just after mid-night. "On the count of three, gimmie a big push Courtney", Dr. Bailey said. After three strong pushes, they heard a loud cry. The baby had popped out with ease and the parents had started crying out of joy. "It's a sweet girl", the nurse said as the two parents looked at her confused as hell. Before they could question Dr. Bailey spoke, "Oh, what is a surprise, Mrs. Murphy dear I need you to push on my count.". Not knowing what was going on Courtney began to protest. "There is another baby trying to slide into this world you got a two for one deal going on today", he said with a reassuring smile. "TWINS!!!!", Donald and Courtney yelled together.

Two short minutes later, their baby boy came rushing into the world eyes open wide. "Oh, my Gawd! Its 2 of them", she said tiredly.

Courtney and Donald named their daughter Champeia Denise Murphy. She was a beautiful, unexpected 5 lbs 2oz surprise that they were both in love with already. Champion Danarious Murphy was a whopping 6lbs 8oz. The new parents stared at their creations in awe. "I didn't give you your dream wedding, but I did manage to give you a 3- day celebration. You have Valentine's day, the twin's birthday, and your birthday. We definitely about celebrate every year." Donald said smiling. Courtney just nodded, "Best birthday gifts a girl could ask for". "Thank you, Queen Bean. I love you beyond words", he said as he kissed her face Courtney had drifted off to sleep still groggy from the drugs. Donald made it to the waiting room to tell the waiting family about the additional baby. Everyone was so excited and could not wait to see the bundles of joy. After 24 hours of observation, the mom and babies were released to go home. Sabrina and Vernetta planned a family gathering, things were in full swing. Lots of food and even more desserts. Everything is in place and ready for the new family to arrive home. The grand mothers were willing to fight everyone for the babies, including the parents.

Alvin silenced the room. "Congratulations bro. You and my sister are the best. I am proud of you". Everyone started clapping but he kept talking. "Dacember baby. I will take whatever you give me, but I want twins too. I can't let little bro out do me". It took a minute but the news of Dacember and Alvin having a baby finally set in and the news definitely didn't go over the way he wanted it to. Caz was ready to jump on Alvin. Being the voice of reason and the only person unfazed by the news was Sabrina, she spoke. "So yall mean to tell me that yall didn't know they was fucking?", She said with a smirk. "Them two been fucking like rabbits for a while now. Why you think Dacember go missing so much, she was two streets over getting folded like a lawn chair". "Ma!", the girls yelled at their mother's candid way of speaking. Laughing, "No seriously. I had my suspicions but one day the heffa pocket dialed me and I heard them breathing like fat kids with asthma after a marathon and calling each other's name.". Dacember's face turned beet red. "Don't be embarrassed now mama. Your ass was not shy when you were getting folded up like a pretzel", Sabrina laughed at her daughters' expense. "Alvin don't get too comfortable, I'm still in range to fuck you up". Sabrina then winked at Alvin. I love you just like I love Donald and I know you will do her right." Everyone began congratulating the two on the upcoming baby. Donald threw his hands up at Alvin saying, "Damn bro we got secrets now". Alvin dropped his head feeling like he was the little brother.

During all the commotion the doorbell rang, and Sabrina answered seeing Detective Jennie on the other side. "What the fuck you want?", Sabrina said with much attitude, but she peeped the skinny jeans and tight yellow fashion nova shirt with matching heels. "Hello Sabrina. Is Chelsea here?", Jennie answered. At that moment Big C came around the corner. "I got this ma", as she stood in front of her mother. Sabrina walked away slowly being nosy. She needed to know why the damn detective was at the house. A few minutes later Big C walked into the room holding Jennie's hand. "Chelsea, I don't know what you are smoking but we don't fuck with 12, so she not welcomed here". Sabrina said ready to cause a scene. Big C tried to speak but you could tell she was nervous. Jennie acted first. She grabbed Chelsea by her head and tongued her down Infront of everyone. The entire house got silent. Nobody knew what to say or do. "Well, I wasn't expecting that", Courtney said with a laugh. Rolling her eyes, Sabrina walked over to Daddy T who was laughing at his woman. "Yall bitches stay with surprises". Sabrina started holding her chest like Fred Sanford, "Pinch me somebody. I think this the big one". After everyone stopped laughing. Sabrina was hugging her child, letting her know that her decisions was fine with her. "Damn C, out of all the bitches you could have had, you got jammed up with the police, no wonder your ass always played cops and robbers growing up." Sabrina said. Big C laughed with her this time as she shrugged her shoulders. Donald whispered loudly to Courtney, "She must not have done a background check on Big C", but they do say opposites attract". Everyone balled into laughter, the tension was officially gone from the room. The party continued and everyone had a good time. While fixing plates Caz said, "You know we family now Ms. po-po lady, so that means no arrest can be made with in the family circle. We have immunity". Beauty joined in and said, you gotta earn your black card too, cook chitterlings, and Support Black Lives Matter". "You down", Sabrina said with a raised eyebrow. With a huge

Kool-Aid smile Jennie said, "DEAL!". "Aye daughter in law, Daddy T screams across the room "I got this ticket right, I need you to be I dream of Jennie and blink a few times to make it magically disappear". "Can you handle that". Jennie laughed and nodded. Everyone started talking again. Big C managed to pull her girlfriend away from everyone. "You sure you want to do this. There is no turning back after this." Jennie kissed her again. "After five years on the force and two as Detective, I think I will survive". The two looked at the family with love. "You got my back right partner", Jennie asked. Big C put her arm around her, and answers "Definitely"!

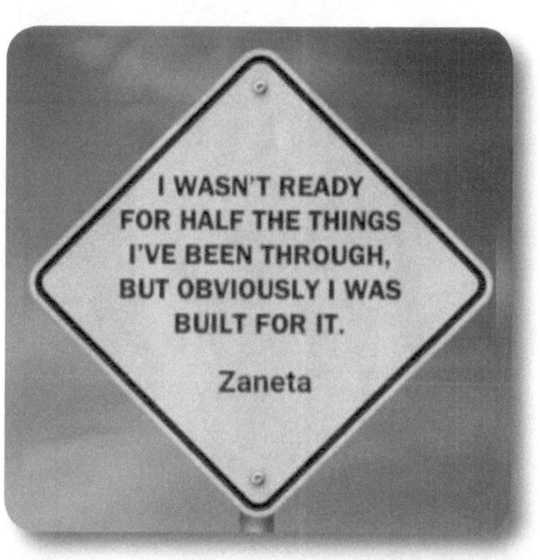

I WASN'T READY
FOR HALF THE THINGS
I'VE BEEN THROUGH,
BUT OBVIOUSLY I WAS
BUILT FOR IT.

Zaneta

i am Zaneta

Life has forced me to sacrifice my happiness for the benefit of other people. These experiences have taught me to look at life differently and to be more open to other ideas. My life may not have gone in the direction I had hoped, but I am grateful for all the lessons I learned. I still have dreams, they're just not what I expected them to be.

THE END!!!!!!